Son
of a
Preacher Man

Son of a Preacher Man

My Search for Grace in the Shadows

JAY BAKKER,

Son of Jim and Tammy Faye,
with Linden Gross

HarperSanFrancisco
A Division of HarperCollins*Publishers*

HarperCollins books may be purchased for educational, business, or sales promotional use. For information please write: Special Markets Department, HarperCollins Publishers, Inc., 10 East 53rd Street, New York, NY 10022.

HarperCollins Web site: http://www.harpercollins.com
HarperCollins®, 📖®, and HarperSanFrancisco™ are trademarks of HarperCollins Publishers, Inc.

FIRST EDITION

Library of Congress Cataloging-in-Publication Data

Bakker, Jay.
    Son of a preacher man : my search for grace in the shadows / Jay Bakker with Linden Gross.—1st ed.
        p. cm.
    Includes index.
    ISBN 0–06–251698–1 (cloth)
    ISBN 0–06–251699–X (pbk.)
    1. Bakker, Jay.   2. Bakker, Jim.   3. Messner, Tammy Faye.   4. Children of clergy—United States—Biography.   5. Evangelists—United States—Biography.   6. PTL (Organization).   I. Gross, Linden.   II. Title.

BV3785.B29 A3 2001
269'.2'092—dc21
    [B]   00–059719

06 07 08 09 RRD(H) 10 9 8 7 6 5 4 3 2

To my wife Amanda
  Your love is the most important thing to me on this earth

And to Jesus,
  Thank you for never giving up on all of us

We can rejoice too, when we run into problems and trials, for we know that they are good for us. They help us learn to endure. And endurance develops strength of character in us, and character strengthens our confident expectation of salvation.

ROMANS 5:3–4

Contents

Contents

Acknowledgments

A Very Special Thanks to:

My Dad

I am so grateful for all the love and wisdom you have given to me. I am so sorry for all that you have gone through. I wish I could have traded places with you. My goal in life is to love and forgive people just like you have. Dad you are truly my hero and it is an honor to be your son.

My Mom

Mom you are so special to me. We are two of a kind. You are such a good friend and an even better mom. You always make me feel like I am at home no matter how hard things are. You have shown me that it is okay to be who I am and for that I will always be grateful. I love you with all my heart.

Tammy Sue Chapman

Sissy, we have made it through this strange journey together. You are the only one who knows what I've been through. The bond we share is so very special. I could not have made it without you. I love you and poo bear loves you too.

James and Jonathan
I love you guys very much. May the force be with you always!

Thanks to:

Bo Julian
Thanks for being there for me during the hardest time of my life. I could not have made it through everything back then without you.

Donnie Earl Paulk
Thank you for being the brother I have never had, but most of all for showing me who Jesus really is.

Scott Steward
Thanks for the comedy. We will always be best friends.

Tommy Stamps
You will always hold a very special place in my heart.

Matt Douglas, a.k.a. Ricardo Tubbs
We sure had fun. I miss those days.

George Gardner
Thanks for the smiley face pancakes, and getting me to school on time. I love and miss you.

Miss Burke
Thank you for believing in me!

Mike and Heather Wall
Thank you for all you have done for me, especially helping make my dreams come true.

Jackie Thompson

Thank you for helping me get my life back together.

Steve Brown

Thanks for writing *When Being Good Isn't Good Enough*.

Gloria Instone

Thank you for taking care of me in the middle of the night.

Vi Azvedo

Thanks for always being there.

Dr. and Mrs. Jackson

Thank you for all your help.

Randy Renfrow

Thanks for being there when I needed a friend the most.

Liz Perle

Thank you for believing in my story and making this book happen.

David Bazan

Thanks for writing such honest music and allowing me to use your song in this book.

Arinando Saavedra

I am very happy that you are a part of my family.

Tornado Tattoo Wrecking Crew: Gary, Bob, Ryan

You guys are good friends. Thanks for the tattoos!

David Brokaw

Thank you so much for believing in me and my family. You made sure this book happened and I can't thank you enough for all you do.

Linden Gross
Thanks for doing an amazing job on this book and helping me to put the past behind me.

Brennan Manning
Thank you for your message of Grace. It has brought me closer to Jesus.

Kate Marsh
Thanks for the great article in *Rolling Stone.* It made this book possible.

Rolling Stone Magazine
Thanks for printing such a positive article, and giving me the title of my book.

Mike Young and Carlene Julian
There are way too many things to mention, but thank you for every one of them.

Shirley Fulbright Martin
You are truly my second mom. Thank you for always being there for my family.

Bobby Murray
Your friendship and love for Christ means the world to me.

Bishop Earl Paulk
Thank you for believing in restoration and openly standing up for the Bakkers when most did not.

Bob and Molly D'Andrea
Thank you for the home and job, and taking me to visit my dad during the hardest time of my life.

Phillip Bray

Thanks for giving me the chance to minister and allowing my dreams to come true.

Justin Green

You are one of my best friends, and I truly believe that God is going to use you in an amazing way.

Kelli Miller

I am so glad God allowed us to share the same dream. You are truly loved and family to Amanda and me.

To all the PTL Partners

Thank you for making PTL a reality and sharing in our lives.

Gregory Fisher

Thank you for being the one to help me get my life back!

Don and Clariece Paulk

Thank you for opening your home to me and making me feel part of the Paulk family. Your love healed much pain.

Pastor Phil and Faith Shaw

Thank you for being there for my family in our darkest hour.

Ray and Faye LaForce

I will never be able to thank you enough for all that you have done for me and Amanda, and my family.

Revolution staff: Dara, Kevin, Bethany, Julie

Thank you for all your hard work, but most of all for loving people the way each of you do.

All the people who are part of Revolution

You are all very special to me.

Safe House Family

It is an honor to serve with all of you.

Kennie Myus

You are such a good friend. Thank you for your selfless service to Revolution. God has great plans for you to fulfill your dreams, and I can't wait to see it!

Steven Schoenbacchler

Thanks for your friendship and teaching me an important lesson in life.

Chris Gilbert

Keep on spinning in the free world! Thank you for keeping me sane in Phoenix.

Larry, Sheila, Michael, Paul, Stacy

Thank you for allowing me to be part of your family. I love you guys very much.

The Lucky Devil Atlanta

Thanks for letting us take the pictures for the book in your amazing store with your amazing people; especially Suzie.

Introduction

People have said that I have had a prodigal son kind of life. Maybe. But what I know for sure is that I have spent time in my personal wilderness, and I've had my share of tests. I would go through it all again, however, if it meant I would be the recipient of the AMAZING grace of Christ. I guess that, more than any other reason, is why I decided to tell my story now. I, who have been through the mill, enjoy a sense of peace and purpose today not generally associated with people who look like me. I feel strongly that it is my responsibility to share some of that peace with other people who may feel they just don't fit in.

Writing this book was torture for me not only because I've had to relive the past but also because I have dyslexia. But I feel it is important to give back some of what I have learned about being lost and being found, about anger and forgiveness, about being an outcast and finding peace.

I spend my days speaking and preaching about God to all types of people, including kids who don't feel accepted. Every day my friends and I try to pioneer a new type of ministry. One that reaches out to punk rockers and those who have been labeled "generation x'ers"—a generation so "nothing" in a way that they didn't even give it a name. My generation has gotten kind of lost. We watched our heroes change, our music change, we saw Kurt Cobain take his own life. We witnessed the Columbine shootings. We have tattoos, piercings, and we listen to music others find bizarre. We feel different and we act different. We are definitely a different type of generation trying to make our own way and our own impact on the world.

I've been able to do that in large part because of God's grace. Grace for me is the unconditional love of Christ that all people need to understand. It is through grace that I have found strength in the toughest situations, like my father being in prison and my family being ridiculed. God has allowed me to make it through my parents' divorce and through watching, what I felt was, the whole church turn its back on my family. I survived the humiliation of my dyslexia, my alcoholism, my drug addictions, and being a high school drop-out.

I discovered grace by going through all the events that you'll read in this book. I had to lose a lot. I had to watch my family lose everything. I had to watch my family fall apart. I had to go through a hard time, but it was all worth it when I realized God's unconditional love for me. It doesn't really make sense that I wouldn't trade any of the unhappiness for what I've learned, and the experiences that I've had. But there it is. And I know it's useful.

I certainly know a lot about what happens when people turn on each other. It is the plot line of my life. I have seen my family made fun of on *Saturday Night Live*. I have heard preachers who have the ears of millions say things about my parents no one should ever have to hear. I should have just cursed God and died, because watching the people I loved most being ripped apart by their fellow churchgoers was hell. But being able to stick through that and endure made me realize how amazing God truly is. It is time to put the bitterness to rest and to take a look at ourselves, especially in the church, and ask, "Am I being Christ to another person?" or "Am I destroying another person", "Is the church destroying the church?"

It's horrible what's happening in the church today with so many pastors, church clergy, and members of the church being destroyed over petty things and infighting. I believe that we've given sin its power back, as I will discuss this much further in *Son of a Preacher Man*.

I want this book in a way to serve as a warning tool and as an example of the dangers of what happens when we play political and religious games in the church. It does destroy people, and we have to stop destroying one another especially as the body of Christ.

Anyone can have access to the strength and dignity that I have found, and that message is why I have written this book—as a testament and as a book of overcoming, a book of encouragement, a book that can make a difference no matter how hard your life is, no matter what you're going through. I hope that this book will also reach out to teenagers and young adults and all the people who tell me things such as, "I can't do anything with my life; I'm just a nobody." In my ministry, people have said to me, "I don't know how to read or write"; "I dropped out of high school"; "I'm an alcoholic"; "I'm a drug addict"; or "I'm covered head to toe with tattoos and no one will ever respect me." I encourage them and say, "No matter what you've been through, you can make it."

I want people to have the hope I've found. I want those who are struggling with drugs to read this book and know they can have a happy ending, I want the fifty-year-old tattoo artist who has never felt God loved him or accepted him to know God really does care. I want the doubting preacher to feel like there's hope. I want the pastor in a small town who doesn't know if God loves him, to feel encouragement and strength through this story. I want people to say, "You know what? We've got to stop tearing each other apart and start restoring one another."

I hope this book can help us realize that we're human and we all make mistakes and none of us are perfect, so we can stop trying to better the church by condemning other people, and better the church by concentrating on ourselves.

The answer to that lies in this: Love makes us truly free. Christ has made me free, and we are all free in Christ, no matter who we are or what we have done. No matter what our sin is, no matter what our struggles are, God loves us. It seems our country has been obsessed with scandals, but we've forgotten about the people on the other end of those scandals, the people we are talking about, the people we are allowing to be scandalized, and the pain and the hurt that they go through. I hope people will read this book and get an insight of what it feels like to be going through a scandal, what it's like to hurt, what it feels like when people hate your family, and what it's like to feel lost and alone. Not so people feel guilty, but so people will change their hearts and change their minds and say, "You know what, I'm not going to judge them so harshly next time," or "Next time I'm going to write a letter of encouragement, or pray for that person, or do whatever it takes to build up those people, instead of add to their unhappiness."

This is a book for any person who has never felt good enough or who has never felt accepted. If you've felt broken, lost, like an outcast, rejected by God, as if God hates you, rejected by the church, rejected by the world, alone and devastated, and as if no one understands you, then this is a book for you.

This book is not written to put the church down, it's not written to put people down—it's just the book of my life, my testimony, and what I've gone through. I feel like I've lived through all that I have so God could use me to help bring hope to a hopeless generation and help bring unity back to the body of Christ and to the church. For me this book is just the beginning of a ministry and a beginning of a life—a very successful beginning at that—because through all of this mess, I realize God loves me no matter what. I am holy and blameless in his sight, and I would not trade that for anything in the whole world. I hope you enjoy this book. As my father always used to say, "God loves you, he really does." Thank you.

Jay Bakker
February 2000

PART ONE

EDEN

1

The Keys to the Kingdom

If anyone had an excuse to lose faith in God, it would've been me. I'd been beaten up so often by traditional religion that turning away from God, as so many others my age did, would have been the most natural reaction.

I started life on Christian television. You would think that, based on my family, some of the most influential Christians in the world, I would have led an exemplary life. As it turns out, I wasn't so different from other pastors' kids, who are notoriously rebellious. After all, we have pretty high expectations to rebel against.

The gospel my father preached and my mother stood for is often flattened out by others to one of material riches. I hate that. My parents' real message was always about prosperity of the soul: charity, love, forgiveness, and respect for others. Unlike so many other ministers, they believed that only God had the right to judge. But I lived life in the shadows of that ideal.

Yes, my family did things wrong. And so did I. It would be a long time before we would get back to the light. In the shadows where we walked, I would see many dark things and meet many dark people. Along with my family, I experienced the dark side of a Christian message that no one should ever have to endure. I lived through the dark side of my parents' marriage, which ultimately did not stand the test of time or hardship. And I dove headlong into the dark side of myself.

Considering how my life began twenty-five years ago, on December 18, 1975, that's a far cry from how things were supposed to play out. The doctors had told my parents that my mother would be in labor with me for at least eighteen hours. So my dad, per my mom's wishes, went ahead as usual with his TV ministry show. But when the doctor was forced to perform a cesarean and cut me right out of my mom's belly, Dad was still on camera. As soon as the program directors got word that I'd been born, they flashed "It's a boy! It's a boy! It's a boy!" across the screen. I think the TV audience knew I'd arrived before my dad did.

Having millions of television viewers share my life would be the norm for me for the next eleven years, for I was basically born into the premier family of a megamedia church. I was required to appear on TV with my parents every Sunday for church services, every holiday, and anywhere from twice a month to five times a week on top of that.

It was an amazing time in Christian America. My father was at the forefront of a group of men and women who forever changed how Christ's message was received. He, like Oral Roberts, Robert Schuller, and Billy Graham, among others, found a way to broadcast sermons to millions from coast to coast. And in the process, people began to look to him for guidance. In short, our lives revolved around my parents' television ministry, called PTL, which stood for "Praise the Lord."

I guess we were supposed to be the perfect Christian family. But even though my parents openly discussed some of our problems on camera, things weren't really what you'd think.

PTL was my father's dream, one he worked hard for. My mother and father's ministry had come a long way from handmade puppet performances on Pat Robertson's fledgling Christian Broadcasting Network, their life a long way from hanging their own wallpaper in a one-bedroom third-floor walk-up rental apartment.

My parents weren't born into the abundance I was. My mom grew up poor in rural International Falls, Minnesota, with a mother who was ostracized because she had divorced, a loving stepfather who worked at the local paper mill, and seven younger brothers and sisters she had to help care for.

They kept their clothes clean with a wringer washing machine, depended on an icebox instead of a refrigerator, and, despite twenty- or thirty-below-zero winter temperatures, had to use an outhouse instead of an indoor bathroom.

My dad's family had a little more money, but not much.

My parents met in North Central Bible College in Minnesota, where they were both studying for the ministry. They married soon after, on April 1, 1961, left school, and became itinerant evangelists. Mom played the accordion and sang, and Dad preached. During Sunday school, they would perform a puppet show for children: Mom provided the voices and action for Suzy Moppett and Allie the Alligator, while Dad stood out front and talked to the puppets.

In 1966, that show landed them on Pat Robertson's new TV network. The audience loved them, and what was supposed to be a one-time appearance became a regular feature. The puppet show's success also led to Dad's hosting a Christian TV show called the *700 Club,* which he had modeled after Johnny Carson's *Tonight Show*. The talk show proved an instant hit, and the station's viewership and donations soared. Since the new television ministry didn't sell advertising, its existence was completely dependent on donations. And with this new format, TV religion began to sweep across the nation and eventually around the world.

After eight years, Mom and Dad moved away from Pat Robertson. After helping found TBN (Trinity Broadcasting

Network), they launched PTL. Their show was so popular in Charlotte, North Carolina, where they'd moved, that Dad decided to buy time on some fifty stations—one station at a time—across the country to see how it would do nationally. The overwhelming success that washed over them seemed heaven-sent.

Indeed, throughout their careers God had provided for them whenever they were in need. This was no different. PTL grew 7,000 percent in its first year and a half. The rise was so swift that there was no way to accurately chart the TV ministry's growth projections.

The money that followed this growth allowed my parents to build Heritage Village, a miniature reproduction of Colonial Williamsburg, complete with red brick buildings, a steepled church, and landscaped grounds. By 1978, Dad had his own satellite network (one of only four in the world), with over twelve hundred cable systems carrying his show into 13 million households across the country. (At its peak, nine thousand cable systems and two hundred broadcast stations would be connected to that network.) It seemed obvious—God wanted them to thrive.

My parents didn't invent the gospel of prosperity. Oral Roberts and others started preaching that God wanted His people to live well in the 1950s. The message took root and became almost a tradition, especially in the charismatic movement. "God wants you to prosper" became almost as common a message as "God wants you to do good," "God loves you," and "Rock 'n' roll is the devil's music." With his satellite network, Dad was simply spreading the word to more people than ever before. And because they liked what they heard, his ministry reaped the financial benefits. Meanwhile on Wall Street, of course, prosperity was taking off in another direction. It was the perfect religion for the time.

The world at large has focused on my parents' preaching of prosperity, but as I sat in their room late at night and listened to them talk while playing with my little toy action figures, my men as I called them, I heard a different message—one of forgiveness and the abundance of God's love. In addition to preaching that on TV, they put their beliefs into action. I remember my dad always seating a mentally handicapped man in the front row, focusing on him, and periodically hugging him. When a little girl was abandoned at the church, my parents brought the toddler home and took care of her for a day until the mother returned to pick her up. They could have pawned her off on any one of a thousand employees or passed her over to the authorities. Instead, they incorporated her into our family and probably would have adopted her had her mother never shown up. And when vandals burned an African American church down, Dad made sure its parishioners got the funds they needed to rebuild. He even sent his own staff to quicken the restoration. His goal was to make PTL a place where anyone with a need could walk in off the streets and have that need met.

Strangely, especially since we were considered by many to be the first family of Christianity, I don't remember my parents talking to me about religion or even reading me stories from the Bible. It was as if I'd absorbed the gospel through my skin during Dad's sermons.

When I did think of heaven, I pictured big white clouds, mansions, and streets paved with gold (I suppose because gold's deemed our most precious material on earth; God's kingdom would be so wonderful that we would be able to metaphorically walk on gold!).

Hell, on the other hand, could be summed up in a single word: fire.

And grace? That was just a song.

Like any good Christian kid, I went to Sunday school and was a member of the Royal Rangers (the Christian equivalent of the Boy Scouts). Between those experiences and the many speakers I was exposed to at PTL, confusion was bound to arise. I remember one of the guests who came on my parents' show announced that Smurf dolls were satanic. I had given my sister a bunch of Smurfs as a present—she threw them back in my room so the devil would get me instead of her.

My Sunday school teacher preached a lot about the rapture, stressing that if we did something wrong, Jesus would take everyone but us to heaven upon His return.

"Are you going to be ready when Jesus returns, or will you be left behind?" he regularly questioned.

I remember coming home a couple of times and panicking because the house was empty. Frantically running from room to room in search of my parents or my sister, Tammy Sue, or anyone else, I would think that Jesus had taken them all away and left me behind because of something I'd done or neglected to do.

Despite the theological discrepancies and lack of overt teachings from my parents, I basically took for granted the fact that I loved Jesus, just as I took for granted the fact that my parents were just about the biggest pastors in the country.

That alone shaped my life in ways that I'm still not completely aware of.

Growing up in the religious limelight and having over one hundred death threats every year meant full-time bodyguards almost from the moment I was born—we even had a guardhouse at the entry to our Charlotte home that was manned twenty-four hours a day—plus a housekeeper and a maid who were like family, groundskeepers, and people at PTL who gave me anything I wanted.

Ironically, though we were held up by many as the Christian family ideal, I didn't always experience *that* firsthand. Though my parents loved my sister and me, like so many other parents these days their busy lives tended to get in the way of how much time we could spend together as a family. In addition to the television show they did together, my mom taped a second PTL show called *Tammy's House Party*. Dad not only functioned as a pastor and managed PTL's multiple ministries, he basically turned himself into an urban planner. (The scope of what he accomplished still amazes me.) By the time I was two, Heritage USA, the sprawling Christian retreat my dad created, which would become the nation's third most popular attraction, was already being built. I was five when it opened to the public.

During the next six years, my whole life would revolve around that magical Christian retreat and entertainment facility, which included a state-of-the-art TV studio, various ministry buildings, hotels and motels, campgrounds, a residential subdivision of vacation and retirement homes, shops, restaurants, tennis courts, a pool, and a roller skating rink. I even attended school on the grounds. And though our house—Tega Cay—was about fifteen minutes away, Heritage USA served as my backyard, my playground. My friends and I rode motorbikes around its twenty-two hundred woodsy acres, and we ran around the Grand Hotel playing the *Miami Vice* version of cops and robbers. The gospel according to Sonny Crockett, brought to you courtesy of PTL!

Back then I wanted to be Don Johnson, who played Sonny Crockett, so bad it was ridiculous. I had my hair cut to look like his, wore sports coats over pink or peach T-shirts, and even had a shoulder holster with a toy gun that looked real. My friends and I would set up fake drug deals. I would load Ziploc bags with flour and put them in a duffel bag, and we'd go buy tons of fake money at the general store in Heritage USA. We'd wrap stacks of cash and put them in another bag. I was always Crockett, and my friend Matthew was always Tubbs. So we'd set up the drug deal, with our other friends playing the bad guys. As soon as we made the exchange, we'd pull out our guns and yell, "Freeze! Miami Vice!" and then chase the "perpetrators" around Heritage and inside the Grand Hotel, screaming around corners and scaring little old ladies almost to death. My dad would routinely reprimand me, but I think it kind of tickled him a little bit.

I had it all.

The keys to the kingdom.

2

Shadows

Despite a life of material abundance, I too was on a spiritual quest. The millions who watched my family's daily broadcasts felt as if they actively participated in my growing up, and in a way they did. Every year six hundred thousand of my school pictures were mailed out to people across the country. But the kid behind the pictures, even though he didn't know it at the time, hungered for spiritual satisfaction. I wanted the love my parents preached. But between being in either the shadow of PTL and Heritage USA or the glare of the spotlight that shone on my family, I had a hard time connecting up with that message.

I had always felt different growing up, and it didn't all have to do with who my family was. Though I had every toy a kid could ever want, I never felt I was quite good enough or that I fit in. For starters, I had become overweight. I really didn't like to see myself on television or in all those pictures we would have to pose for as a family. "Man, I look so fat," I would tell myself. So I was a target. "Hurry up and get your fat ass up here," my friends would say when we played. When kids weren't making fun of my weight or the money my folks had or how I dressed, they made fun of the warts on my hands. Every night I would pray, "Lord, take my warts away." Eventually they did disappear, but not before I had grown into a really insecure kid with almost no self-confidence.

I can remember frequently leaving my neighbors' house in tears because the teasing was simply too harsh. I was the pudgy kid who always questioned whether we should really be doing something and who always fell and got hurt when he did dare to do something, like riding a bike off a ledge. Of course, if I ever stuck up for myself, my buddies would get angry and we'd get into a fight. Most of the time, it was easier to leave.

Of course, I was also a kid who had everything he could want in the toy department. Until my parents finally pulled me aside for a stern chat, I could charge anything from Heritage USA to my parents' account, and I was not above tendering bribes of pizza, drinks, candy bars, and new toys in order to get the cool kids to hang out with me.

Still, the only people I really felt comfortable around were adults. My bodyguards, who became part of my life almost as soon as I was born, rated near the top of that list. I carried my own security badge they had given me. Though they occasionally had to deal with incidents like the bomb threat in 1985, which forced us to flee to a hotel for the night, and the hundred-odd death threats the family received every year, for the most part they functioned like family.

Tommy Stamps, whom I've known since I can remember, was one of my best friends. A mustached, slender Magnum P.I. look-alike, Tommy taught me how to throw a football and didn't hesitate to give me a charley horse and tell me to stop acting like a goofball whenever I was a brat. "Where's my hug?" he would ask at the end of each day. I really loved him. Though he was paid to be with me, I know he loved me too.

When I wasn't hanging out with my bodyguards, my schoolmates, or my daredevil neighbors Darren and Ryan Bycura, I usually played pretend with my little men—some five hundred four-inch-tall GI Joes, superheroes, and Transformers, as well as *Star Wars* action figures—for company. No matter what or where, I'd have had two of them in my hands and another two in my pockets at all times.

Even on the TV set, I'd have my men right behind one of the throw pillows on the set's couch, just out of camera range. While my father imparted his words about God's love, I'd try to forget that I was on television, secure in the knowledge that, with my old play clothes already on underneath my nice suit, I could be back outside thirty seconds after the cameras stopped rolling.

"I'm going to get you!" I'd murmur, imitating shots being fired or Superman flying around until my father would grab me with a stern command to stop. I'd agree, and then keep going at it.

I didn't question my lack of piety. I let myself be carried away by my imagination, and by my men. Unlike my parents or any of the others around me, my men did not make me put on a show for anyone. I didn't have to please them or do anything for them. I could just be myself, and they accepted me 100 percent.

Despite the sense of loneliness that I never really acknowledged even to myself, I thought we were a close family. Of course, I never saw my dad and mom before school. A security guard named George would usually wake me up, make me breakfast—my favorite was pancakes with Mickey Mouse ears and a syrup smile—drive me to school, and then pick me up. But I thought that was normal.

Every night my folks made a point of coming home for dinner unless we ate out as a family. Dad even established an ironclad rule that we all had to be home by six-thirty. We'd sit at the dinner table and eat whatever Johnny May, our Southern maid, had whipped up. After dinner, I'd watch TV with my parents, while my sister, who was six years older than I was, played rock 'n' roll downstairs. When the music would get too loud, Dad would stomp on the floor to get her to turn it down. Mom would make popcorn or fudge, and the three of us would climb in their bed, munch, and talk.

But my dad was a workaholic, so that regular family time didn't last too long. Heritage USA was his life. Of course, it had to be his first priority if he was to bring in the necessary funds, along with keeping the huge operation running.

The only time he really relaxed and hung out was on our houseboat or on weekends with our neighbor Dr. Blair Bycura, a top podiatrist and father of two, whose idea of a good time was going out to drink and smoke cigars. Though Dad rarely drank, they found common ground. Together, they'd tinker with one house or the other or dream up something to do for their kids. One year they decided we needed a playhouse. So they built a two-story structure on stilts in the trees between our two houses, complete with glass windows that opened and shut, a mini-refrigerator, window-unit air conditioner, and ladder escape hatch. Another time they dug a trench down a hillside and built a plastic water slide for all of us. Dad nearly ripped his ankle off on a protruding root on one of his runs.

On Sundays, Dad would open up "Jim's Bar & Grill" for our weekly poolside barbecues. All the neighbors—including the Bycuras—would come. And though there was never any liquor, there were plenty of hot dogs and burgers. Steaks were out. My parents have always preferred simple food and simple restaurants like Pizza Hut, Red Robin, and Kentucky Fried Chicken.

At least once a week, my mother would take me shopping with her. I was so in love with her when I was a little boy! (I still am.) I would just play on the dressing room floor while she tried on clothes at the mall. If I was good, I'd get a new toy. Then she would take me to Pizza Hut. I would sit up on the ledge in the booth, Mom would cut my pizza up, and we'd talk as we ate together. We were such tight friends, and I was so used to being with her all the time, that I cried nonstop the first time she put me in nursery school. After less than a week, she gave up and took me out, whereupon I resumed being her constant companion.

Although I may have been a mama's boy, I definitely revered my dad. He was my hero, this huge pioneer of Christian television with one of the largest churches in the country, who sat with presidents, was a regular visitor to the White House, and built amazing sand castles complete with secret passageways with his son. Though he was often melancholy and brooding, he seemed like Walt Disney to me, a visionary who was determined to make Christianity exciting to adults and youngsters alike.

I wanted to be just like him. Unfortunately, I was too young to realize that he would never have been able to live up to the ideal of him I created in my head, an ideal reinforced by a relationship that was, oddly, both extremely close and terribly distant.

Since security guards were always with us, we never spent much time alone together. When Dad would prepare his sermons in his home office, I'd go down and play alongside his desk. Mostly, though, I'd tag along behind him as he walked through the Heritage USA grounds with his entourage.

Even before a single structure had been built, he saw it all. "The amphitheater will be here, and this is going to be the front of the hotel. Here's our suite, and your room will be right here. The shopping's going to be over there. There will be a toy store, and an ice-cream store named after your sister," he'd tell me. "This is where the petting zoo will be. We'll have a chicken, a cow, you'll even have your own horse, and you can name him whatever you want."

He made me feel as if I was part of the creation of this whole world. And I was. I helped him pick out the merry-go-round for Heritage USA as well as the miniature train that took people around the grounds. By taking me to the shows and seeing what I liked, he could gauge what other kids would enjoy.

Eventually it got to the point where I too could envision what the buildings would look like. Later, as the framework was being erected, he would take me back, give me a little hard hat, and walk me through the structural skeletons. Then, in record time, the buildings would be finished, with more on the drawing board.

He even showed me where the $13 million water park—which would become Heritage USA's claim to fame and ultimately contribute to its downfall—would be. He took me around the artificial island and 25-acre lake as they poured the concrete, and later let me test the 163-foot slide that ran down the "mountain" before the water park opened.

"Son, get a shovel," Dad announced when one of the pools had gotten filled with sand during construction. Together we shoveled that sand out. That was one of many things that showed me how much my dad really believed in this place. He wasn't just paying people to build it; he was doing his part to make sure that things were done right. Once Heritage USA opened, Dad would ride around its four square miles with a tape recorder, noting every burned out lightbulb or unkempt flower bed. Like Mayberry, everything had to be perfect.

But it wasn't, at least where I was concerned. Despite the money and everything that came with it, something was clearly missing.

To really understand my dad—and me—you have to understand the time. The influence of evangelicals had risen to the point where they had been a determining factor in the election of presidents Jimmy Carter, Ronald Reagan, and George Bush. Their influence extended from the officials in office to what children were reading in school.

Toward the end of the 1970s, televangelism had hit its all-time peak. Preachers like Oral Roberts, Robert Schuller, Jimmy Swaggart, Jerry Falwell (the originator and head of the Moral Majority), and, yes, Jim Bakker became household names as they each tried to carve out a different niche for themselves. While Roberts and Swaggart fell into the more emotional, tent-revival strain of Christianity, Falwell preached a more fundamentalist theology. Dad, who was third-generation Assembly of God, attracted viewers from both ends of the spectrum, which helped his appeal. But, boy, did he pay for his success.

For starters, since there were no commercials to fund the show's production or the purchase of airtime, he had to solicit that money during each show. As the show's popularity increased, so did that cost for airtime. Add to that the expense of building and then running Heritage USA, which at its peak attracted six million people a year. In short, Dad had to raise a million dollars every other day just to keep everything afloat, from the television show to all of PTL's ministries. Sadly, that became his focus after a while. He had to feed the monster or risk losing it.

He admits now that he may have lost sight of God in that need to feed the work of PTL. But there was a lot of ministry going on at Heritage USA, and there was a lot of PTL money going to build missions, schools, and hospitals all over the world.

In many ways, PTL became a powerful ministry whose progressive actions helped thousands and thousands of people. It created Fort Hope, which provided homeless men with shelter as well as job retraining in order to help them get back on their feet and regain productive lives. Heritage House gave unwedded pregnant women alternatives to abortion by providing them with a place to live as well as a twenty-four-hour hot line, prenatal care, professional counseling, adoption services, and the opportunity to pursue their education or work part-time. A nationwide network of almost a thousand People That Love centers distributed free food, clothing, and furniture to the poor. Heritage USA offered drug and alcohol abuse programs and marriage counseling in addition to eighty religious services a week. PTL provided thousands of Bible-study courses to inmates as well as hundreds of free TV satellite dishes to penitentiaries across the country so they could receive our broadcasts. And $52 million was sent out to other ministries led by people like Franklin Graham (Billy Graham's son) and Oral Roberts as well as others less well known.

Dad was basically doing the work of fifty full-time ministers. But when it came time to judge him, people didn't look at any of that. They saw the water park, with its Raging Canyon Rapids that you could run on inner tubes. They focused on the giant waterfall, behind which lay a café, and the wave-maker. "If the Bible says we are to be fishers of men, then a water park is just the bait. And I don't see anything wrong with using pretty fancy bait," Dad told his television audience.

His followers agreed, sending money to help build it. But others like the Reverend Jimmy Swaggart hated him for that water park. I'm not sure why. Maybe they thought it was worldly or that Christians weren't supposed to have fun.

Actually, once you factored in the costs, which included utility bills of $1 million a month and salaries for a staff of two thousand, nothing really made money at Heritage USA—at least not enough to keep it going and keep Dad on the air. He was just trying to give Christians a place to get away to where they could relax, recuperate, and worship.

But Heritage USA and the water park weren't the only reasons people were gunning for my dad. By the mid-1980s, his television satellite network with its enviable multitude of affordable long-term cable contracts, had become its own kind of bait to televangelists like Jerry Falwell, who was then paying $14 million a year for airtime. A great deal of money and influence was at stake, and the competition among the televangelists for viewers' souls and contributions got increasingly cutthroat. In the crossfire of ambitious rival preachers who felt almost duty-bound to air each other's dirty laundry in the press and on the airwaves, the unrealizable image of the Bakkers as perfect Christian icons almost had to come tumbling down. Although my parents never set out to foster that image of themselves, because of it we would lose everything.

• • •

If he had listened to my mother, Dad would probably still be leading PTL right now. But he wasn't about to do that. My parents' marriage had been dicey for years, a fact they discussed openly on their show. In 1979, after two years of marked marital difficulties and a platonic involvement with a man she'd fallen in love with, Mom left Dad. They got back together and tried counseling, but it didn't help. A year later, she had an affair. My dad's fifteen-minute tryst with Jessica Hahn on December 6, 1980, was, in his own words, a stupid attempt to make Mom jealous and win her back. Getting even was simply a side benefit.

Ironically, my mother didn't find out about Jessica until the rest of the world did some nine years later. Following the poor advice of a marriage counselor, Dad chose to say nothing out of fear that my mother would divorce him. In the interim, my parents somehow managed to stay together. But life wasn't exactly perfect, a fact that exploded in our faces in January of 1987.

Right after breaking ground for PTL's replica of England's Crystal Palace (which would have been the country's largest church seating 30,000 people) on one of the coldest days I can remember, we had gone to our vacation home in Gatlinburg, located in Tennessee's Great Smoky Mountains. Dad was desperate for a break from the insanity that was always part of Heritage during Christmas. Mom, who fell ill during the groundbreaking ceremony, would have preferred not to go out of town. Tammy Sue wanted to stay home with her friends. But, eager to get out of school, I pushed like crazy. So we went. I felt guilty about that for a long time and blamed myself for what ensued.

Though work had forced my dad to return to Charlotte, Mom and I stayed on in Gatlinburg with Vi Azveto, our friend and my godmother (who functioned like a wise mother or grandmother toward me) and the head of PTL's counseling services. Then my mom got the flu. In an effort to calm her symptoms, she mixed Ativan, a tranquilizer originally used to ease her fear of flying, with Aspergum and Valium and promptly overdosed.

Of course, I didn't know any of that. I just knew that something was really wrong, especially when she went out on the balcony to wash her hair, even though the temperatures had plummeted below freezing.

That night I slept in her room. Early the next morning, she started hallucinating. First she saw pink elephants in the room. Then she started to panic.

"There's something in the closet!" she screamed.

Terrified, I jumped to my feet.

"In the name of Jesus, I rebuke you," I yelled.

That was all I knew to do at eleven years old—rebuke the devil out of there.

"That's good. That's exactly what you should do," my mother said approvingly.

I thought she was proud of me and that I had solved the problem. But during the next day she got much worse. From my room across the house, I realized I could hear the TV program she was watching. She had taken a combination of drugs that temporarily made her go deaf.

Vi called my dad.

"There's something wrong with Tammy," she said. "You need to come back quickly."

Instead, Dad had us call a doctor we trusted from the Palm Springs area, where we had a third house and spent a lot of time. Doctor Nichols flew out to examine Mom.

"We've got to get her to the hospital right away," he announced.

It was decided that Mom should enter the hospital in Palm Springs, where my parents knew the doctors, instead of opting for one of the local facilities. So we loaded up and headed for the plane. Once we were airborne, I stretched out on the floor.

"Jamie, get up! You've got bugs crawling all over you," Mom shrieked. "Now get up! The bugs are crawling all over you."

"Oh God, what's happening?" I asked.

Despite her strange behavior over the past few days, I didn't know she was hallucinating.

"Mom, there's no bugs on me, I promise. There's no bugs

on the floor. There's no microscopic bugs, there's no any kind of bugs on this floor."

Next she thought she saw orchestras playing.

"What's wrong with my mom?" I later asked Dr. Nichols, who simply explained that she was sick.

As it turns out, Mom was sicker than anyone knew. After years of medicating herself with over-the-counter and pre-scription medications, she had become addicted to all of them. When she arrived at the hospital, the amount of Valium they had to give her would have killed a truck driver. At the hospital, they brought her down slowly, so her body wouldn't go into shock or suffer horrible withdrawals. Had we waited a day longer, she would have died, the doctors there told us. As it was, they warned that brain damage was a possibility.

When Mom was well enough, they moved her into the Betty Ford Clinic. She only lasted a day as an inpatient. To my mother, a twenty-eight-day in-house rehabilitation program was simply not an option.

"No way," she said the moment we got there.

Then things got ugly. Distressed at being penned in, she carried on all night. Then she begged Dad, who had left the show to join us in Palm Springs, to spring her and let her go home, but continue the program during the day.

Twenty-four hours later, the staff reluctantly agreed to allow my mom to attend as an outpatient.

Mom wasn't the only one to enter the Betty Ford Clinic.

"Hi. My name's Jamie, and my mom's addicted to over-the-counter drugs," I told the recovery center support group in a voice that betrayed how scared I was. I had gone from vacation to incarceration, and all of a sudden I was in a room seeing broken and hurting kids for the first time in my life. It was another dose of reality, which had been hitting me pretty heavily already.

My mom, dad, sister, Vi, and I moved to a new house near the clinic that had a very high wall around it. Little did we know that we'd soon need those walls, because we'd be surrounded by hundreds of press, who then rented these big U-Haul trucks so they could stand on the roofs and shoot down into our home. The three networks all brought their own trucks, complete with direct satellite uplinks.

But more changes would hit before then.

Unable to take the intensified family tension and the lack of interaction that Mom's stay at Betty Ford had engendered—or to bear being separated from her boyfriend—Tammy Sue ran away.

"You're not really going to marry Doug, are you?" I challenged when she told me she was going to leave and marry her boyfriend.

"What do you think this is?" she countered, showing me her engagement ring.

She was sixteen.

Though we had serious dog-out fights while growing up, my sister was still my best friend. It wasn't just that we had shared the same bedroom till I was nine. We'd prayed together every night before going to sleep. Whenever I got scared, I'd jump into her bed. Whenever she got scared, she'd make me do the same. I dreaded going through this circus surrounding my mom's illness without her.

I begged her not to leave, and then tearfully begged her to come back. Even so, she stayed in Charlotte and married Doug without my parent's approval, in a ceremony that none of us could attend.

Dad, however, was determined to be at Mom's side through this ordeal no matter what. So he announced to his TV viewers that he would not return to PTL until Mom was completely well.

The picking was ripe.

3

Betrayed

There's a drawing at the back of a picture book about my parents and the ministries of Heritage Village Church that shows an artist's sketch of Heritage USA fully realized. It's titled "The dream never ends." I hate that illustration. Because the dream, however imperfect, did end, smashed by the ambitions of another televangelist who had lost sight of God.

I was eleven when the *Charlotte Observer,* having learned about Dad's transgression with Jessica Hahn, made it public. Three years earlier, Hahn had called the newspaper and the offices at PTL to accuse my dad of raping her. Knowing that a public admission would lead to Dad's destruction or at least being banned from the pulpit for two years, Reverend Richard Dorch, PTL's general manager, opted to buy Hahn's silence with a payment of $265,000—$115,000 to be split between her and her representatives and $150,000 to be put into a trust fund that would be hers in twenty years as long as she kept quiet. Dad didn't even know about the payoff; Dorch just took care of things.

Somehow, word got out anyway. The *Charlotte Observer* reporter Hahn had originally called had tracked the story down and was about to go to press. Jimmy Swaggart, a fellow Assemblies of God minister who had made a career of publicly condemning PTL and Heritage USA, and Jerry Falwell got wind of "the Jessica Hahn incident," as they called it, from someone who had talked to the reporter. A letter written by Swaggart suggested that the newspaper was about to expose the sexual encounter and subsequent payoff, which would bring down my dad and PTL right along with him.

Dad knew that PTL's corporate bylaws made him PTL president for life and specified that if he could no longer serve, the Assemblies of God would own PTL's operations. Since Swaggart was essentially the top preacher associated with that organization, that implied that he would take over PTL, which he had long been rumored to covet. Dad was immediately suspicious.

Enter Jerry Falwell. There was only one way my dad could protect himself from the Jessica Hahn fallout and a hostile takeover engineered by Jimmy Swaggart, Falwell argued. Dad needed to temporarily resign from PTL for thirty to ninety days, just long enough for Jerry Falwell to talk to leaders like Billy Graham and together go to Jimmy Swaggart and convince him to back down.

It seemed like the only solution.

Dad could no longer put off telling my mother about his fifteen-minute affair.

Mom cried for days, first about the betrayal, then about Dad's decision, of which she totally disapproved. Of course, since I was young, they tried to shield me from what was going on, but I could tell that something was wrong.

At first I thought that people were stressed because my sister had just run away from home. I didn't really start to figure out what was happening until one afternoon when my mother and I were having lunch at a Red Robin in the Palm Desert Town Center along with Eddy Azveto (Vi's husband), Doug Oldman, and his wife, Laura Lee.

As usual, the adults were talking among themselves and paying no attention to me. That was how I got most of my information in those days. I'd either be lying on the floor watching TV while my dad talked on the phone or riding in the backseat of the car while business deals were being discussed.

Suddenly, my mom got real quiet. She leaned over to her friend Laura Lee.

"Jim's going to resign from PTL," she announced in a low, nervous voice. "I don't think he should do it, but he's decided that he has to step back for thirty to ninety days."

"Why is Dad going to give PTL away?" I blurted in a panic.

PTL was all I had known. That's where I went to school, that's where I played with my friends, that's where my mom and dad worked—they had built it.

"Oh God, what's going to happen?" I wondered.

Within a week, the whole world knew about Dad's indiscretion and his decision to leave the ministry. The story attracted a storm of media. TV camera crews, reporters, and photographers shooting down at us from their rented trucks besieged our house. Determined to foil their attempts, we hung sheets over the floor-to-ceiling windows, darted under the house's big eaves when media-type helicopters flew over. When we would go outside we used the back instead of the front entrance, and lay down in the backseat of the car whenever we came and went.

At Dad's request, I took pictures of the photographers to show people what they were doing. I would dress up in one of my superhero or Darth Vader costumes, hide behind trees and rocks, and then jump up and snap a photo of them. They always shot back. So I'd prop up my Darth Vader mask with a stick. Then, while they trained their cameras on that, I'd sneak over to the other side of the compound wall, pop up, and catch them by surprise. Then it almost seemed like a game. But it was a game with brutal stakes.

Dad pulled himself together long enough to make a media announcement. May 1, 1987, was bright and sunny. From the entrance of our house in Palm Springs, flanked by my mother and me in my sweatpants and jean jacket, my dad did what he had to do. His heart may have been breaking, but instincts took over. He chatted with the press, sympathized with their having to withstand the desert heat, and then told the world of his resignation.

He had a harder time dealing with my questions than the press's.

"Daddy, will I be able to go back and get my toys?" I asked.

He had no answer.

If possible, we were judged even more harshly by the very people we might have expected to support us. I'd turn on the TV and see pastors preaching against my parents. All the big guns who had surrounded my dad turned on him with words of judgment and destruction.

"Jim Bakker is a cancer on the body of Christ," exhorted Jimmy Swaggart.

"Jim Bakker is getting what he deserves," moralized Pat Robertson, the man who wouldn't have even had the *700 Club* TV show if my dad hadn't come up with the idea and then hosted it for over seven years.

Less than a week after publicly resigning from PTL, Dad was defrocked by the Assemblies of God.

Despite the storm, we tried to convey the sense that the Bakker family remained united and strong. And in a way we were a little bit stronger. With what seemed like the entire world poised against them, my parents bonded a bit more. Though my father had just admitted to an indiscretion, they seemed closer than they had in months. But they were in for yet another test that would try them even further.

At Falwell's request, Mom and Dad sat down in front of the video cameras to explain the whole situation to the PTL partners, those people whose contributions had helped build PTL and Heritage USA. Then they sent the tape to Falwell. On it my dad had confessed to a fifteen-minute affair. But Falwell's people edited out the words "fifteen-minute," so that it would sound as if he'd carried on an extended affair instead of having a one-time assignation. To this day, it's hard for me to understand why a man of God would do such a horrible thing.

Those Christian attacks paled, however, in comparison to the national television coverage of our family. Daily network bulletins were supplemented with hours of coverage by CNN and *Nightline*. Even Johnny Carson joined in. Though I was no longer allowed to watch TV, I managed to anyway. I'd tune in to hip shows like *Saturday Night Live* only to see them making fun of the two people I loved most in the world. Suddenly it was cool not to like my family.

Even people who had worked for PTL and who I'd perceived as our close friends were suddenly denigrating my dad on TV and talking about how they'd turned their back on him in favor of their wonderful new boss, Jerry Falwell.

"How can these people say these things?" I asked Don Hardister, my dad's bodyguard, whom I'd always looked up to like an uncle. "I can't believe all these traitors. They're all just a bunch of idiots!"

"Hey, Jamie, don't you say that," he snapped. "Don't say that about those people."

At the time, I thought his defense of them was really odd. In time I would figure out that he too had sold out; in one of the most devastating defections, Don would eventually abandon us for Jerry Falwell, for whom he may have been working all along.

Though that's just my suspicion, there's no questioning Jerry Falwell's subsequent manipulations. Years later, Don would apologize to me on my twentieth birthday and give me his badge. I cried.

By late spring of 1987, just a few weeks after temporarily resigning, Dad called Falwell to say that he was ready to return to PTL. Falwell had other ideas. In keeping with the times, he had staged a corporate takeover, pure and simple. Where was the grace in that?

I saw my father cry for the first time ever during that conversation.

"What have you done?" he asked, the tears streaming down his face. "You said you would return this place back to me."

When Falwell refused again, Dad's concern turned to the PTL partners. My mom has said that Heritage USA was my dad's mistress. That's not true. Those TV viewers were my dad's mistress. He loved those people so much.

"Don't you *ever* speak negatively about the partners," he commanded once when I had griped about a guest in the Grand Hotel.

As I see it, Dad wasn't obsessed with building an empire; he wanted to build a place for the partners. And when that was threatened, he didn't worry about the structures or the property. His thoughts turned to the people he'd cared about for so many years.

"You've got to take care of the partners. This is their place," he pleaded. "You've got to make sure you take care of them."

In Romans 11:29, it says that God never takes away a person's call, never revokes it. That's why there's such a need for people to be restored, healed, and returned to their church and leadership when they do fail.

Jerry Falwell did not respect that code.

In an effort to justify a reprehensible power play, Falwell launched a series of televised character assassinations on my father. On repeated news broadcasts, he accused my father of homosexuality (one of the most devastating charges that could be leveled at an evangelical minister and the farthest thing from the truth), thievery, and a unrepentant heart—things he could have no idea about. If his fabrications were designed to tear my father and mother apart, they did their job. But they weren't the only victims. Tammy Sue and I suffered right along with them.

Falwell did whatever he could to make our family look bad, including setting us up only to knock us down again. At one point he told my parents he wanted to help them out by keeping them on salary and providing them with a staff.

"Just create a wish list and write it down," he said through Roe Messner, who was functioning as his messenger at that point (and who would be my future stepfather!). "Then we can negotiate it."

So my mom and dad wrote down all the things they would like to have. Falwell took that list and read it verbatim on TV, claiming that these were my family's demands and neglecting to mention the fact that he had asked for the list in the first place.

"This doesn't seem like a repentant heart to me," he declared.

I was devastated. Falwell seemed so proper and so stern in his suit, with this big red drape hanging behind him, as he stood in the pulpit surrounded by all these other "businessmen." There they were, posing as the Christian Right—as representatives of all Christians—bringing wrongdoers to justice. What a horrible moment in the history of Christianity! It was a bunch of garbage. And it certainly had nothing to do with Jesus.

There's no question that my father made some mistakes. He's the first to admit that. He even wrote a book titled *I Was*

Wrong, which details our whole downfall. But he didn't steal money and didn't defraud anyone.

The theological pettiness of others, along with their lust for power and plain old greed, destroyed my father's ministry, just as it's destroying the church today. As Jesus said in John 16:2:

> *For you will be expelled from the synagogue, and the time is coming where those who kill you will think they are doing God a service.*

As soon as Dad realized that PTL had been stolen, he almost went catatonic. He would lie curled up in a fetal position at the end of the couch, listening to ministry tapes of pastors preaching and gospel music recordings.

Scared as hell, I thought he was dying. In fact, he wanted to die. He refused to talk. And he refused to fight. He just lay there like this fragile, broken man.

Something did break in my dad the day he realized PTL was gone, because he truly, passionately cared about the partners. Frankly, I think he was more concerned for the partners, staff, and ministries that would suffer than he was with his own reputation. It was as if he knew that the dream was over and that its demise would eventually cost the thousands of people that PTL helped every day.

My dad constantly went out of his way to reach out to the

poor, the hurting, and the needy. He had built his whole life on that. I think that's why he became so successful. Sure, he became a little jaded with having to raise so much money and always having to keep up a persona. But my father was genuinely a good man. Even after we'd lost everything, I can remember him taking me to buy a turkey and Christmas toys, including a bicycle, for a very poor family in California. Mom, Dad, and I spent our holidays with them. There were no cameras there. We weren't trying to manipulate anybody. That was just what my folks wanted to do.

When I *really* realized we had lost PTL and that Jerry Falwell wasn't doing us a favor as he'd originally claimed, I called Tommy, my personal guard, whom I loved so much.

"Tommy, I don't know what's going on. We've lost PTL. I'm scared," I said, bawling my eyes out. "Please, fly out. Come out and see me."

I begged so hard he finally agreed. But the head of security, Don Hardister, as I later found out, refused to allow it. And since he was in charge, Tommy stayed where he was, and I remained alone, my parents too devastated and shell-shocked to pay me any mind.

Even after Dad was removed from PTL, things only got worse. Part of Falwell's power play included stripping my father—and by consequence us—of everything we owned. For starters, we were forced to move out of the Tega Cay house. (Though that house was the parsonage and therefore owned by PTL, we had moved into it after giving the ministry another house we'd been donated.)

Having completed the Betty Ford program, Mom, Dad and I flew back to Charlotte to pack up our home. Several reporters had found out about our flight back, possibly from an insider tip, since several of our most trusted friends and personnel were now selling information about us to the tabloids. So a number of reporters bought tickets and traveled along with us, trying to interview us en route. All we wanted to do was to lick our wounds.

Upon our arrival, hundreds more members of the press had gathered at the airport. The gate was so crowded that airport officials had to bring portable stairs to the plane instead of letting us exit the normal way. A car met us on the tarmac and drove us straight out of the airport. My sister and a dozen devastated family members and friends—along with even more press—greeted us at home, where the security gate's wooden bar that controlled automobile access to the property had been removed. We were quickly overrun and overwhelmed.

I was devastated by everything that was happening, more so than people realized. I would go to my friends' homes, and their parents—who had worked for my family and loved them—would trash my parents to my face. Kids repeated the accusations of wrongdoing they overheard their parents make. We were being abandoned by people with whom we'd shared our whole lives.

An old postcard from my parents' kid show, *The Jim and Tammy Show.*

Here I am, playing
around on the set of
their show as usual.

My mom and me at a family dinner. I always thought I had the prettiest mom in the world. She was definitely my first love.

My mom and me in Switzerland. Whenever my parents went out of the country, for business or pleasure, they were sure to take my sister and me along.

My eleventh birthday party. This is one of my last memories of PTL.

Here I am with my favorite bodyguard, Tommy, and my best friend, Matt, in our *Miami Vice* tuxedos, celebrating my parents' twenty-fifth wedding anniversary.

My favorite picture of my parents, taken back at PTL.

One of many family publicity shots sent out to our supporters. This picture was taken when PTL was at its height.

(Top right) Me in my chubby days with my new skateboard. Even back then I was always trying to challenge people; hence the skeleton on my skateboard.

(Bottom right) This picture of my mom, dad, and Aunt Donna was taken for my grandfather when my dad was in the Rochester prison.

My dad and me, putting on our best tough-guy faces at the
Rochester prison.

Overnight, friends I'd grown up with weren't even allowed to play with me anymore. It was really a hard and lonely time. I had just lost everything I'd ever known, and there was no one I could turn to. Even my sister was gone. And my parents were too mired in their own nightmare to help me deal with mine.

My family's world had just been swept from underneath our feet, shattered and destroyed. Since I had heard and believed everything we worked for—respect, love, forgiveness, and the mercy of God—I felt completely bewildered.

Over the next few days, as we packed everything from dishes to toys, security guards treated us like criminals. They slashed boxes we'd already sealed to check what we were taking. They marked all our furniture with big black Magic Marker numbers, because Falwell had said he wanted everything in the house accounted for.

Nothing was too petty for him, it seemed. Claiming that some of our personal property had been bought with ministry money, Falwell even confiscated certain items, which he actually auctioned off from my dad's pulpit. That was like spitting in our face. It seemed as if he chose those things he could make fun of or make the most fuss over, like the yellow electric 1930s replica of a mini go-cart that my father had bought me and my parents' bed.

He even auctioned off our doghouse, which despite all its notoriety was simply a little brown shed in which an old air-conditioner and heater window unit had been installed to keep the dogs from overheating in the summer and from freezing during the winter. Falwell had that carried off in front of all the press before we even got home. A photo shows our five dogs just sitting there looking at their house being taken away.

The fact that this was being done in the name of Christ made it worse. No wonder people hate Christians the way they do or think that Christianity is screwed up, when they see us destroying each other.

When the house had finally been stripped of all its furnishings, I sat cross-legged in my room, empty except for an old *Star Wars* magazine I hadn't seen in years, and sobbed.

"Why, God, have you let this happen to us?"

This was our home. The years here represented the only time I'd ever felt that I had a home. Now that was gone. All in the name of Christ. The light was gone. I was alone in the shadows.

After about a ten-month stint in Tennessee, we moved back to Palm Desert. For a year, we became a real family. We lived on a golf course in a small two-bedroom condo. My mom packed my lunches for the first time in my life and took me to school. Mom and Dad bought me a bicycle, and one of the neighborhood kids and I would ride around or go out in a boat. We lived right on a lake at the golf course, so when people hit their golf balls into the slimy water, I'd offer to swim in and get them. Of course there were hundreds of balls and I couldn't tell which one was theirs, so I would just toss them whichever one I found first.

I got a part-time job working at the clubhouse, polishing clubs and taking players' golf bags to their cars for tips. For fun I skateboarded, rode my bike around the neighborhood, and got into trouble riding golf carts around with one of my new pals. I almost felt like a normal kid.

That lasted almost a year. If we'd stayed in California, I doubt that anyone would have come after Dad. Mom didn't want to leave. She knew I was finally happy in school and that we were functioning as a family for the first time in many years. But as before, my dad had other ideas, which became finalized when Dexter Yager, a friend and supporter who had made a lot of money through Amway, offered us the use of his estate in Pineville, located fifteen miles from PTL.

"I really feel as if God's guiding us or telling us to go back," Dad announced one day.

And that was that. We packed up the van, rented a few U-Hauls, and drove back to Charlotte, where our memory was still alive, if not well.

Though Falwell did whatever he could to erase that memory—including bulldozing all my mom's record albums and anything else with the name Bakker on it into an eight-foot-deep pit in the ground—the Bring Bakker Back Club had launched its operation by then. Its offices looked like campaign headquarters, complete with JIM AND TAMMY, WE LOVE YOU and BRING BAKKERS BACK bumper stickers and pins. They even had JAMIE AND TAMMY SUE, WE LOVE YOU bumper stickers. As thousands of participants worked to reinstate my parents at PTL, my dad tried to get back on his feet by starting a TV program at the Yager Estates, where we lived. In addition, we rented a movie theater near the mall so we could do church services. Attendance grew quickly, to the point that we were forced to relocate to a nearby roller-skating rink.

I tried to start over as well, by finding new friends and new pastimes—like smoking cigarettes, which made me feel safe, and drinking. I knew it was wrong—but I wasn't so sure Christ cared anymore. How could He, with all we'd gone through? I was mad at the world and at the pious one particularly. I'd even sneak out for cigarettes with one of my dad's cameramen. We had a signal: we'd hold our hands way out, which meant "I could go for a cigarette this big." Then we'd go out back to smoke and chat. And as my life seemed to fill, my soul emptied.

I did regroup with some of my former crowd. We'd get an older friend who drove to take us out and buy us wine coolers and beer. Then we'd go back to where he worked, and we'd drink. Now I was finding a religion that worked for me!

One I could trust. I hadn't even turned thirteen, and I was already getting drunk.

There was no way I'd ever manage to live up to the image of the ideal son, so what was the point of trying? God simply made a mistake when He created me, and that mistake's name was Jamie Charles. The way I saw it, I had nothing to lose.

4

Trial and Tribulation

There was to be no stability. In March 1989, after just a few months back in Pineville, a change in zoning regulations stopped Dad from broadcasting. Once again, we had to relocate. This time, we were offered a minister's seven-bedroom lakeside house in north-central Florida to broadcast from. We lasted only two months before moving again to facilities in Orlando.

Mom and Dad had found a Spanish-looking place to rent. The first time I walked in, the house—with its white walls and carpets—seemed strange, almost mysterious. But after so much darkness, it also seemed to symbolize this really big, brand-new adventure that my family was about to embark on.

I was euphoric. I knew nothing about the grand jury investigation into PTL's fund-raising and spending, which, in

December 1988, would lead to Dad being indicted on twenty-four counts of fraud and conspiracy. The charges boiled down to a case of overbooking—having more lifetime partnerships, which came with a guarantee of three nights and four days lodging at Heritage USA, than could be accommodated. Of course, a new hotel tower with five hundred new rooms was just ninety days away from completion. In addition, people were told that availability was not guaranteed and that they would have to make reservations ahead of time. Besides, PTL had always had a policy that people could get their donations back at any time. More to the point, the lifetime partnerships had always been designed to support all of PTL's activities, not just the construction. But none of that was factored in. Indeed, the jurors were never allowed to see Heritage USA for themselves. In short, even though my parents' salaries were determined by a board of directors and even though my parents donated all their book and album royalties ($8 million in PTL's last three years alone) back to PTL, Dad was tried on his lifestyle, not on the facts. Indeed, he was never found guilty of stealing a dime. But within a year, Dad—already convicted on all twenty-four counts—would be in prison.

At the time, however, it simply seemed as if things were back on track. The family had been reunited. My sister and her husband, Doug, were with us. Even my cousin Rhonda had come to help out. Dad was back on TV, shooting a new show—which featured guests like Mercury Morris from the

Miami Dolphins—from a little strip mall. A lot of people from the old show had returned, including Dale Hill, Dad's director, who had also been a neighbor at Tega Cay. I worked as a cameraman.

Florida, however, did not greet us with a huge, welcoming embrace.

Pastor Book, a Christian extremist of the Church of Christ in Orlando, had spearheaded the protest against Universal Studios when *The Last Temptation of Christ* came out. Now, with my father in his backyard, he gathered his troops again. This group of ultra-right-wing conservatives targeted my mom and dad. Book, along with members of his congregation, paraded a coffin outside my dad's new church to protest our being there. BURY JIM AND TAMMY read the terrifying sign draped around it.

My dad's not a fighter and rarely confronts anyone. But the sight had upset me so much that he actually went out and asked Pastor Book to leave. The latter refused.

On the flip side, a local radio station brought Jessica Hahn into town and was threatening to bring her dressed in a skimpy outfit to my parents' TV studio. They did bring her to a bar just a few stores down from our makeshift studio.

I just couldn't understand why people hated my family so much. Of course, the people who hadn't liked us originally still didn't. As before, local radio stations would make fun of my mother and father, and the newspapers continued to attack my parents' ministry. But being hated because we were humans and had made mistakes was something totally different. Where was the Christian love?

Still, we tried to live a seminormal life. Dad and I would go to the movies together. Sometimes my friends would come visit from Charlotte, and my dad would take us to the all-ages club on Pleasure Island so we could go dancing.

Every once in a while, portents of the storm that was gathering would flicker. In Charlotte, for example, somebody had brought us a videotape about how to testify at a trial. But mostly, we all simply ignored that upcoming reality, almost until the trial date itself. God just wouldn't let anything terrible happen.

Dad's trial started on August 28, 1989. And although Jerry Falwell's bid for power had cost my family its stability and my parents an empire they built out of nothing, it quickly became apparent that he was not the only one with an agenda.

If the trial had been held outside of Charlotte, I don't think my father would have gone to prison. Or if only the jurors could have gone to PTL and seen the type of place that was built there and where the money went. But with the judge—known familiarly as Maximum Bob for his tendency to hand down maximum sentences—presiding, none of that would happen. The judge didn't even try to disguise his feelings. I remember seeing him put his fingers in his ears as a videotape of my dad interviewing Billy Graham on his TV show was played for the jury.

At the beginning, I went to court with my father every day. During the recesses, I'd sit with the lawyer and eat the Oreo cookies and cheese that were usually set out.

My sister was having a real hard time going through the trial, so in the courtroom I would do whatever I could to cheer her up. Once I put quarters in my eyes and looked over at her, to try and make her smile. The judge wound up mentioning that to the press. He never understood that I was trying to lighten things up. I just didn't want her to be sad. Instead, he even threatened to hold my sister in contempt if she didn't stop crying after Dad's verdict was announced.

Everything we said or did was fair game in those days. While at the hotel in Charlotte, I invited a bunch of my guy friends up to my room. Noticing that you could rent a dirty movie, we decided to watch the free thirty-second sneak preview. Then we decided to watch it again, not understanding that the mere action of playing it twice confirmed its rental. When the promotion didn't go off after thirty seconds, we realized our mistake.

"Oh, no! What do we do?" we wondered in a panic.

I cut the movie off quickly and didn't say a word about it to anyone. A few months later, the *Enquirer* reported that my dad had watched a porno movie in his room. Of course, Dad came straight to me, and I denied the charge. I'm not sure I've told him the truth to this day.

It was weird how closely members of the press watched us, how willing they were to tear us apart, and how even the people at this top hotel were selling us out for a price. At that time, you could get quite a bit of money for any story that had to do with the Bakkers. A tabloid actually offered me, a thirteen-year-old kid, $30,000 to do an interview.

As the trial progressed, I remember feeling that the attorneys weren't doing much for my dad. Even at my age, I couldn't help noticing that instead of bringing in key people from the organization who could discuss financial dealings and intent, or even the auditors who had poured over PTL's books for ten years, they simply brought in a lot of partners or fans.

When the trial hit its third week, I was sent back to Orlando so I wouldn't miss any more school. My folks had enrolled me in school at a church called First Baptist because the head of the school had worked at PTL. The teachers at this ecclesiastical school, however, didn't make things any easier on me. Though I was having a tough time for obvious reasons—bursting into tears in the middle of a class—they were really hard on me and even belittled my family and me. I spent most of my time in the school counselor's room, located just down the hall from the sanctuary of the huge church the school was attached to.

I also had serious academic problems. Reading and retention were fine and comprehension has always been a strong gift, but when it came to spelling I was hopeless. No matter how hard I tried, I could never envision the letters of a word in the right order. So I'd just sound it out in my head and write it phonetically.

Testing finally revealed that I had dyslexia. I wouldn't find out what kind until I was nineteen, well after I'd dropped out of high school. But the learning disability diagnosis did explain why I often felt so stupid when confronted with schoolwork.

Exams were the worst. I remember breaking down while taking a math test. As I stared at the questions, it was as if the test itself were taunting me.

"You have five minutes," it seemed to say.

I couldn't do it. Terrified, I froze. Then I gave up, got out of my chair and started for the door.

"Jamie, if you walk out of this room, you fail," the teacher told me.

"Fail me," I replied as I bolted out of the classroom.

"God, I'm stupid. I'm stupid," I told myself as I ran. "Everybody around me knows how to do this. I must be stupid since I don't."

Unfortunately, many Christian private schools are not usually oriented toward helping kids with academic problems. They're more like college preparatory. You have to be elite and above the cut. So I continued to have a tough time even though they knew I had dyslexia.

Of course, I was also totally confused about how my life had fallen apart. One day, the notion that my Dad really might go to prison instead of just being fined hit me like a bulldozer. I broke down in the middle of class and sobbed. As servants of God, teachers and staff might have been expected to show some empathy. Instead, back I went to the counselor's office.

My own problems, however, took a backseat again on August 31, 1989. That day, the neighbors came to pick me up from school and took me to their house. I knew something was wrong, but I sure didn't know what. There were reporters surrounding my house, and no one would tell me what was going on. They wouldn't let me see the newspapers or watch the TV news. They told me that something had happened with my dad, but wouldn't say what.

Eventually, they snuck me back to my parents' house. When I walked in, Mom looked horrible. Then she pointed to her head.

"Someone shot Dad," I thought in horror.

Then another thought hit. "Maybe he shot himself."

"Your dad had a nervous breakdown," she finally said, adding that I would stay over at a family friend's house while she went to be with Dad.

"Don't worry," she said before getting in the car. "Everything is going to be okay."

That evening, I saw footage of my dad crying, his wrists and ankles shackled in chains as he was led off to a prison mental ward, where he would remain for a week. I was devastated. I would later find out that an acute panic attack while in his lawyer's office had made him feel so sick that he didn't think he could make it to court. Instead of talking to the judge and getting Dad admitted to a hospital, however, the doctors attempted to calm him with a tranquilizer called Xanax. The medication did the opposite, to the point where he started to hallucinate. When he didn't show up in court, the judge ordered that my father—sick as he was—be apprehended at his lawyer's office and returned to the courtroom in chains.

When the story aired on TV, people across the country made fun of my dad's crying. I'll never understand how they could do that. I felt all his pain and more. God seemed nowhere in sight, so I did my best to forget about Him.

I started rebelling in small ways, but instead of providing guidance, my school used my problems as an excuse to distance me. School administrators would send me home because I was wearing a plain T-shirt instead of one with the required pocket on it. When I put a little blond streak in my bangs, they told me not to come back to school until I had dyed it back to its original color. They suspended me for seven days when a second-grader reported that she'd seen me smoking a cigarette in a McDonald's miles away. They even called the parents of this one girl I was dating and told them that she should no longer be allowed to see me or talk to me. If any other kid had been dating her, they wouldn't have thought twice about it.

Here I was going through all this hell along with my mom and dad, and instead of guiding and helping me in what was clearly a very dark time, the religious establishment turned its back. My anger built even more. I can remember at times getting up and punching the wall and screaming at my teacher.

Unable to handle school any longer, I returned to Charlotte to be with my dad during the remainder of the trial. Even so, I didn't face the fact that my dad might go to prison.

None of us really thought Dad was going to go to prison. We knew he wasn't guilty. So, like Dad himself, we figured that God would intervene and bring him through, just as He had so often in the past. I thought that at worst they would just fine him heavily.

I was wrong.

I was in the shower at my sister's home—a trailer in Indian Trail, North Carolina, where she lived with her husband and new son, James—when the verdict was announced.

"Jamie, Jamie, come out here," Tammy Sue yelled.

I could tell she was crying.

"What's wrong?" I called from where I was.

"Dad was found guilty on all counts."

I couldn't believe it. I just stood there, letting the water stream over my head.

"How could they have found Dad guilty?" I asked myself. "How is this possible?"

With sentencing two weeks away, our whole family drove back to Florida. Dad wore my North Carolina hat and slept in the back of the car the whole way. Once there, I took our time together for granted, not understanding what was in store for my dad or for me.

Some things had changed. Every day, for example, I'd go with my dad while he checked in with a parole officer and got drug-tested. But in other respects, life remained the same.

If I had realized that Dad was going to prison, I would have handled that time so differently. But the lawyers were so positive, insisting that he would never spend a day behind bars. And I guess no one wanted me to face the truth.

The morning Dad left to return to Charlotte for sentencing, he knocked on my door.

"Hey, Dad. What's up?" I asked sleepily as he came in.

"I'm leaving," he responded.

Then he handed me a heavy gold-plated ID bracelet. It had his name, Jim, on it.

"Son, I wore this growing up. I want you to have it.

Too sleepy to say much, I hugged him instead.

"Okay, Dad," I said. "I love you, and I'll see you in a few days."

"If I don't come back, you'll have to be the man of the house," he added, his voice strangely husky. "Take care of your mother for me."

"No, Dad," I countered, not understanding why he was getting so emotional. "I'll see you when you come back. I'll see you in just a couple of days."

Then I put the bracelet he'd just given me on my night-stand, rolled over, and went back to sleep. Even if he *was* sentenced to time in prison, I was sure that they would let him come home to put his affairs in order and say good-bye to his family, a standard practice for those convicted of white-collar crimes.

Wrong again. And for the duration of his prison stay, I would feel guilty about blowing him off that morning.

Dad was sentenced to forty-five years—more than most murderers get—and ushered away in handcuffs and leg irons by federal marshals directly from the courthouse. We didn't even know where they'd taken him for two full days, days filled with excruciating uncertainty and fear. I would see him next in a visiting room at Rochester Federal Prison, located in Minnesota, some sixteen hundred miles from our home in Orlando. By then he would already be a veteran who knew how to follow orders and keep physical contact like hugs to a brief minimum. Unable to deal with any more pain, I had delayed my visit for three long months. I knew I couldn't handle seeing him in prison and then having to leave him there.

Even at this stage, the lawyers continued to give me false hope.

"Oh, your dad got forty-five years, but we'll have him out in a couple of months on appeal," they'd say.

So that's what I believed.

"Well, it looks as if my dad could be out in a month or two," I'd answer when asked for an update.

I said that for five years.

PART TWO

The Fall

5

Low-Level Searching

My father's going to prison would mark
the start of my own journey in the wilderness. Here I was,
this thirteen-year-old skateboarding kid who had spent his
whole life growing up at PTL. Suddenly, at the exact time
that the country entered the recession, we'd lost everything. My dad was in prison. We were moving all over the
place. I didn't understand what was happening. And I reacted badly.

I had experimented with alcohol and pot for the first time
some months back. Despite my youth, those would quickly
become the rule rather than the exception.

Carl Jung is supposed to have said that alcoholism is a
low-level search for God. Well, I was sure looking for Him—
in all the wrong places and all the wrong ways.

The heavy partying that would characterize the next seven years started the night my dad was sentenced. I was hanging out in front of my house with a friend, Steve, chewing Ban Smoke gum in an effort to quit smoking. (Having found out about the cigarettes we used to sneak together, our parents had forbidden us to continue smoking.)

Across the street, a party was in progress. A group of guys smoking cigars and drinking beers walked up to us.

"Lord, what do these guys want?" I thought.

"Hey, we're having a party. You guys want to come?" asked a tall, stocky sixteen-year-old jock named Brett Wilkes, who lived in the house across the street.

Then his friend, a preppy all-American type with brown hair and an easy smile, introduced himself.

"My name is Bo. I don't know if you know me, but my mom owns the house you are renting."

His mother had mentioned Bo Foutch to me, and my mother had told me that I should hang out with him.

"But what if this guy's a dork?" I had challenged.

Actually, Bo had said the same thing to his mother. Who would have guessed that he would become my best friend, protect me through high school, and wind up a groomsman at my wedding?

At the party, there were girls everywhere. Our new friends mixed us a drink and gave us smokes. So much for our

resolve on that front! The whole scene struck me as the epit-
ome of popularity and coolness.

"Wow, this is the kind of life I want," I thought. "I want to
hang out with these people."

"Hey, man, we've got to do this again," I told Bo later that
night.

"Yeah, sure. Give me a call," he said.

For the next two weeks, I called Bo and left messages on
his machine.

"Hey, Bo, this is Jamie. What's up, man? You want to hang
out?" I'd ask.

He didn't return the calls. He saw me for what I was: a
little dork skater kid.

At his mother's prompting, Bo finally called during the
middle of the week and asked if I wanted to go to the movies.
I couldn't believe he was allowed to go out on a school night.

"Hold on a second," I said, running across the house to my
mom to ask if I could go.

Even though my academic problems had me on the verge
of dropping out in favor of home school, my mom quickly
agreed. I couldn't believe it. In hindsight, I figure my mom had
called his mom to say that I was depressed and needed a friend.

While Bo was on his way over, I remembered his preppy,
cool look. By contrast, I dressed like a skateboarder, in
raggedy old pants, with whatever shirt was lying around, and

a ball cap. For years, I hadn't cared about what I had on. All of a sudden, however, I desperately wanted to be accepted by Bo and the cool crowd he hung out with.

So I took the only tailored shirt I could find in my closet, buttoned it up, and tried to look as cool as I could.

"What's up, Prep?" Bo asked when he came to the door.

Embarrassed at being caught trying to fit in, I blamed the change of clothes on school pictures.

After the movie, we went for pizza. Despite the age difference—he was entering the eleventh grade and I was still in seventh—we hit it off. It was as if God had given me favor with this guy, because I wouldn't have made it through my teenage years without him. For the first time in my life, I felt accepted immediately.

"I don't care that you're thirteen," Bo told me. "And I don't care about who your parents are. Actually, it's kind of cool."

As we drove back home, I decided to go for broke.

"My name's Jamie, but I've always wanted to go by Jay," I announced. (My dad's secretary, Shirley Fulbright, had a son named Jay, who was about six years older than I and one of the coolest guys ever.)

"Let's start now," Bo said. "We'll call you Jay."

Changing my name was just part of finding the new identity I coveted.

"What about my clothes?" I asked.

"We'll go to the Gap," he replied.

At this time that was the place for any preppy kid to go. The next day, armed with a couple hundred bucks from my mom, I bought a bunch of plaid shirts along with khaki pants and some white ones trimmed with pink and blue. Southern preppy at its worst!

A lot of the kids who ran with Bo were leery of me because I was so young, but they accepted me because of him. It also probably seemed like a novelty to have Jim Bakker's kid hanging out with them.

Suddenly I had a whole new persona. I was done with the old Jamie Charles and PTL. I had lost everything else. The church had turned its back, but these guys were willing to embrace me.

Popularity and attention from cool new friends not only made me feel better; it seemed like the answer to my problems. I thought I just had to change who I was to earn their love.

It would take me ten years of floundering to figure out that I had to come to terms with my past before I could become the man I wanted to be. It would also take me that long to figure out that in looking for myself, I was really looking for God.

At the time, however, I was so desperate to be accepted by Bo's older crowd that I would have done anything. Soon I was partying every weekend to fit in.

"I'm going to drink just as much as they do and go as far as they go," I decided.

The third party I went to, these guys were bonging beers one at a time. They filled a sixteen-ounce plastic cup for me.

"Why don't you pour another?" I suggested, figuring that if I hit two to their one, I'd really prove myself.

I threw up quite a few times that night.

"You're real cool now, Jay," one of the guys said, his voice heavy with sarcasm. "Look at you—you're all throwing up. How cool is drinking now?"

His words only made me mad. I *knew* that drinking was the way to be accepted in this new life I had created for myself and to cope. So instead of heeding his warning, I drank and partied more.

Partying didn't heal the pain. I solved that another way. With my dad in prison, I didn't know how to feel, so I just tried to cut off feeling altogether. That may explain why at one of the worst periods in my life, I felt as if I were finally getting things together. Being liked and accepted was like a drug, a natural high. I wasn't the chubby little Bakker kid everybody made fun of any longer. I was this cool kid. Of course, despite being confronted with tabloid headlines every time I went to the market, I was still in such denial about my dad's being in prison that I hadn't even been to visit him.

My dad had felt blessed all his life. I knew he had to be

suffering. I just didn't know how much. All that God had provided was gone—the houses, the cars, the staff, the stuff, the money, the friends, and the platform.

"Was God gone too?" Dad wondered.

Eventually, being stripped of all the trappings would lead him away from the prosperity message he had once preached to a deeper truth. But at this stage, it just filled him with despair.

"There's no sign of You," Dad cried out to God from his cell. "If You're there, shake the leaf of this artificial plant. Do something to let me know You care."

And now I was gone too. But I simply couldn't face confronting this new reality firsthand.

"Do you want to see Dad?" my mother would ask each time she went. Each time I refused.

"Well, eventually, you're going to have to go see him," she countered.

When I finally did go near the end of 1989, the long-postponed visit confirmed the suspicion I'd tried so hard to escape—that life really was still hell.

Mom and I had waited in line outside in the freezing temperatures before being admitted to a locker room, where we had to take off our jackets and put our shoes through an X-ray machine. After walking through a metal detector, we filled out all this paperwork, which we would have to fill out each and every visit, and had our hands stamped. Then we passed through these huge brown steel-barred electronic sliding doors that crashed behind us as they closed. Caged in a small, overpacked walkway, we stuck our hands under a neon light to show the stamp. Then we just sat there with the tons of other visitors until it was time for the group of five to ten people we'd been lumped with to be called.

I cried the first time I saw him in his prison khakis. He looked like himself, but faded, his complexion and his hair both lighter than I remembered. Even his expression and his manner seemed worn and washed out. And though he looked happy to see me, I couldn't help feeling that he was putting on a positive face for my sake.

It was scary. The prison guards showed no respect for the families, even though none of us had committed any crime. With our loved ones imprisoned, we were going through our own hard time. The guards just made that worse.

Our first Christmas was a real bottom moment. It was freezing cold and snowing, and the waiting line that snaked around the front of the brick prison was extra long because of the holiday. From where Mom, Tammy Sue, and I stood, you could see the two fences topped and separated with coils of razor wire. As usual, few words were spoken, though our shared crisis created a kind of silent, automatic bond between us.

As a concession to Christmas and the crowds of visitors, we all met in the prison cafeteria that day, though it took another couple of hours before we were allowed in. Once inside the orange-, yellow-, and brown-walled cafeteria, we found Dad and lined up for food. Presents were handed out to the kids. I thought they were from the prison itself, but it turned out they came courtesy of one of the prisoners' groups.

We had barely started our dinner when they announced that time was up and we had to leave. As my mom and sister hugged my dad good-bye, I just sat there, paralyzed with fear, confusion, and sheer terror. How could this have happened to my family? How could this be Christmas? Finally, I slammed my fist down into the cafeteria table. Despite its being bolted to the floor, all the trays jumped.

"Jim, hug your son," Mom said.

As he put his arms around me, the tears streaked down my face. It seemed as if the little boy inside me was slowly being killed, a little more every day.

I watched my dad file out with the guards, then threw away the present I'd been given.

"I don't want anything from this place!" I screamed.

On the way out, I guess I didn't quite get my hand under the neon light that sat in the steel cage we had to pass through.

"Put your hand back underneath there," a guard yelled.

"I did," I snapped, shoving it back under angrily, looking as if I were ready to bite his head off.

"You have to sign out," another guard commanded when we got to the main room, even though only kids sixteen or older got to sign themselves in or out, or even visit unaccompanied.

"I'm only fourteen," I replied, with a fresh round of tears. "I can't even sign out. Leave me alone."

A couple of days later, I found out that the guards took issue with my behavior.

"If your son ever raises his voice or acts up again, you will never see him the remainder of your prison term," they told my dad.

The only way I could deal with Dad's being in prison and my life being turned upside down was to escape reality whenever possible. So I indulged in whatever I could to do that, especially upon my return from those visits to Rochester. One night I drank a whole bottle of vodka mixed with Gatorade. Eventually, I blacked out after going onto some guy's lawn and cursing at the top of my lungs at a kid who had made a crack about my parents.

The next day, Bo came by.

"All the guys, we've talked," he said. "They wanted me to come by and tell you we're not going to buy you alcohol anymore. You need to calm down."

That lasted maybe a couple weeks. Before I knew it, we were back in the saddle again, partying.

Having been placed in a class for kids with learning disabilities, I once again felt like an outcast. I could barely stand to be at school. When I was there, the reality of my dad's being in prison and how my parents' life had changed seemed to haunt me. As with any kid who doesn't like going to class, school just seemed to amplify my problems.

So I skipped class a lot. Aware that I was suffering, my mom took me to one counselor after another. She couldn't afford the expense, but I needed to go. I wanted to go. The sessions didn't help. Things got so bad that my mom, who hated conflict and did what she could to avoid it, actually confronted me about ditching.

"What's wrong with you?" she demanded one day while we were in the car. "Why won't you go to school?"

How could I tell her that I was simply in too much pain?

Going to school brought its own difficulties, like the time I came to the assistance of a punk-rock chick with a shaved head who was being harassed by a large teenage boy.

"Listen, man, why don't you just leave her alone?" I said. "You're bugging her, and she doesn't want to deal with you."

He turned to look at me.

"Yo, Jay," he answered. "How does your father like getting it in prison?"

With a scream, I started picking up chairs and throwing them against the wall. Leaping over to him, I pushed him against a glass window and pulled my fist back. Only the teacher's jumping in front of him saved him from being knocked through the window.

"Go! Leave!" she cried.

I continued to yell and scream as I made my way down the hallway. Passing a large trash can, I picked it up and threw it against the wall.

Then the bell rang, dismissing last period. Someone told me that my antagonist took the bus home, so I ran over to where the buses were waiting. At least fifteen of his buddies stood around.

"Where is he?" I screamed, ready to tear this guy to pieces.

He must have known I was crazy mad, because he ran for the bus when he saw me, even though all his friends were there. I chased after him, but was stopped from boarding the bus. All I could do was continue to scream and kick the wall by the parking lot.

The episode earned me a week's in-school suspension. My tormentor fared worse. After I explained what had happened, the school administrators refused to allow him to return to school for two weeks.

Despite the social gains I had made, I still harbored such anger, pain, and sadness. I missed my dad so much. It was as if this huge part of me were gone. Nothing made sense. I didn't care about studying or grades. I didn't care about much of anything, except getting my dad home.

Eventually, the school administrators put me in a weekly counseling session for hurting teens. Suddenly, I found myself in a room with seven or eight punk-rock, Goth, and skinhead kids. Strangely, we all hit it off real well. I could really relate to what they were going through. For the first time, I realized that maybe the only difference between my life and everyone else's was that the whole world was able to watch my family's troubles on television.

Hanging out with this new crowd would actually cause me to have quite an identity crisis. Here I was, this skateboarder-turned-preppy kid who had gone and made his whole life over to be accepted by a group of high-school seniors. Now I was being accepted by kids my own age who were actually a lot like me—the real me. But instead of choosing one clique, I tried to please both. I would be preppy one day, punk the next, or a hybrid of both.

Either way, I partied whenever I could. In addition to drinking, I'd already tried pot when I was in Florida and huffed gasoline with a girl down the block for something to do. But I was about to up the ante.

Bo and I had flown with my mom to Minnesota to visit my dad. As soon as Bo and I got to our hotel room, we automatically set up a party. By now, I had a whole social life in Minnesota—including friends and a girlfriend named Mindy. That night, there was talk about doing some acid.

"Man, Jay, don't do any acid," Bo counseled. So I didn't—then.

We partied our guts out every night we were there. And every morning I'd have to go visit my dad, feeling like hell.

The possibility of Dad's noticing the obvious wear and tear didn't slow me down for a second. Neither did winding up at a kegger way out in the country, surrounded by rednecks determined to beat us up.

Bo watched over me a lot. Even though he wasn't a Christian, he seemed possessed by an angel. When people would come up to me offering really addictive drugs like crack or cocaine and I'd almost have my hand out, he would literally grab my wrist and steer me in a different direction.

"No, man, you don't need to do that," he'd say. "Let's go hang out over there and have a beer instead."

But Bo wasn't always there to save me from myself. One evening, after he had returned home, some of my new friends decided that I should definitely try acid.

"We'll just split a tab in half," they announced. "It won't be a big deal."

I thought the acid would kick in right away. When nothing happened, I went out to smoke a joint, then returned to the hotel's small café for a snack. I had just started eating when all of a sudden I felt as if everyone was looking at me.

"You guys, I've got to leave the restaurant," I said.

Thinking that I had just smoked a little too much weed and was getting paranoid, I went up to the room. A couple of kids came with me and turned on the TV. Before long, I was seeing a rabbit coming out of the back of one of the girls' hair.

"You know what?" I asked. "I think I'm tripping."

I spent most of that night totally freaked out, sitting in the empty bathtub or inside the closet.

The next day, I felt unbearably empty, as if my soul had been raped. Still, I had to get up and go see my dad. So I pulled on a sweatshirt and slicked back my hair. I didn't fool him for a second, especially since I started crying the second I saw him.

"What's wrong with you, Son?" Dad asked.

I couldn't answer.

"I think Jamie's on drugs," my father told my mother later that day.

He was right. Little did he—or I—know how much that would cost me.

By now, my tendencies to self-medicate had become obvious. Still, I couldn't see that I had become an alcoholic and an addict. At fifteen, it just seemed that everyone around me had perfect lives, while mine was so odd and traumatic. Despite my mother and my friends, I felt so horribly alone.

"Has God abandoned me?" I wondered, the few times I even thought about Him.

I knew my sister, Tammy Sue, was suffering as well, and that made everything just that much worse. No one would give her a job, afraid that her being a Bakker would cause them to lose business. Though she had been poised to take off as a singer, with a slated appearance on *Star Search* and her album about to be distributed on Capitol Records, all that had vanished. So had most of her singing bookings. When her husband's paint-and-body car shop didn't bring in what they needed, times got so tough that their water and power would be turned off and they'd literally have to recycle soda bottles to buy peanut butter and a loaf of bread.

Where were the people of our church who we had helped so much before now that we needed them? Where were the people of other churches who could encourage my father and his family? How could men of the cloth write letters to my dad saying that they hoped he got raped in prison?

"If this is God and being a Christian, I don't want to be a part of it," I decided.

6

Alone in the Dark

· · Somehow I didn't fail the ninth grade. By tenth grade, however, Bo and all my other friends who had been seniors had graduated. I was alone again.

I had tried to change my image to fit in, though the little skater, punk-rock kid in me continued to blossom no matter how many preppy clothes I put on. Although my schoolmates called me Bo's clone because I dressed so exactly like him, soon I was adding my own weird touches, like combat boots or my Misfits Fiend Club T-shirt.

For a while I thought I was Jim Morrison—I wrote poetry, wore tight black jeans, little Indian belts, and cowboy boots, and drank, smoked pot, and tripped on acid. But then the punk rocker in me took over again.

Suddenly it was cool to be punk. Nirvana's 1991 album had really changed the way kids viewed alternative and progressive self-expression. I had gotten the message the year before with Social Distortion's album. There was something in their music—and in punk rock in general—that reached out to me and said: "Life is screwed up, and that's okay."

Of course, I was still drinking, smoking pot, and tripping on acid. I just looked different than before.

Not surprisingly, my behavior created substantial problems at home. I had started sneaking out of the house the summer between eighth and ninth grades. Though my curfew was midnight, I'd climb out my ground-floor bedroom window and return to the party I'd been forced to leave.

Mom, who was trying to deal with her own traumatic loss of identity and lifestyle, caught me every now and then. Once she put a lock on my window to keep me in. I broke it in half when I tried to open it with a key I had lying around and went out anyway. I was going to glue it back together, but upon my return I found a Post-it note with an arrow pointing down to the broken lock. "Because of this, you are grounded for four days," the note read.

That didn't stop me. Neither did her nailing my bedroom window shut.

More often than not, I simply wouldn't come home by my curfew and wouldn't call. When I did finally creep into the house at one or two in the morning, I'd find her sitting in the dark.

"Where have you been?" she'd demand, starting to cry. "I thought you were dead in a ditch on the side of the road."

Eventually we made a deal that if I was going to be home after midnight, I would call and let her know what was going on.

Despite these conflicts, Mom and I remained really good friends who loved to talk and go out to the movies or to dinner. I was the first one to jump to her defense if anyone crossed her, even if that someone was a lot larger than I.

"What's your problem, man?" I demanded when a big fifty-year-old biker at a flea market made fun of her makeup. "You'd better apologize."

"Hey, kid, too bad."

I insisted again that he apologize. To his amazement and mine, he did!

"That's right. You're a pretty sorry excuse for a human being," I railed in parting.

Mom, however, didn't know how to control me when I was out of line. She was just too hurt and too overwhelmed with trying to take care of Dad, run the church she had launched in a small Florida warehouse, and restart a ministry. To accomplish the latter, she traveled frequently with Roe Messner, the contractor who had built Heritage USA, looking for a new location where she and my dad could minister and even potentially open up a hotel and restore the lifetime partners.

All that time that Mom and Roe spent together led to talk, including an article in the *National Enquirer* about Mom and Roe having an affair. I wasn't too concerned. I was used to tabloid reporting being all lies. But something, as it turns out, was going on.

Though my sister had an idea that my mom and Roe might be involved in more than just business, I didn't think a thing about it. In hindsight, I remember a few incidents that should have tipped me off, like the day that Mom refused to say where she'd been after having been out a really long time. Her attitude and body language reminded me of mine the times I'd come home after curfew.

Still, I didn't dwell on that. Or them. I was too caught up in my own romantic intrigue. Over the summer, I had met Suzanne, a free-spirited eighteen-year-old brunette. She didn't want to hook up with me at first, or even go out, because I was only fifteen. But I persisted. The relationship that ensued knocked me on my heels.

We dated all through my tenth-grade year, even though she was already away at college in Gainesville, Florida. But every weekend she'd visit me, or I'd go see her. I lived for our time together.

I started seeing less and less of my mom because I'd spend every minute I could with Suzanne. The more time I spent with Suzanne, the more time my mother spent with Roe, as it turns out. I felt guilty about that for a long time, but then I couldn't see past Suzanne. She consumed my life.

My friends also felt left out. "Jay, we don't feel like we see you anymore," they said.

It was true. When Suzanne was in town, we'd show up for their parties, stay for ten or fifteen minutes, and then take off so we could be alone.

The relationship with Suzanne finally came to an end in early January 1992. The distance between us made things too difficult, so I called it off. We both cried when we broke up over the phone. That night I went out drinking with my friends.

"What have I done?" I asked myself halfway through the night. Suddenly I knew I'd made a terrible mistake.

In the days that followed, I was just a wreck. All I could do was listen to sad music. My friends didn't understand.

"Ah, don't worry about it," they said. "Get over it. Let's just move on."

But with school still on top of me, it just seemed as if my life were breaking apart. I felt that if I could just tell Dad how my heart ached, he could help me through it.

"I want to go see Dad," I told my mom.

"Well, you know, Roe would love to take you to go see your father," she replied.

I really looked up to Roe. Not only was he helping us find a place for the new ministry, he was one of the cooler guys I'd ever met. For starters, he had stuck by my dad. (Indeed, when he agreed to a liaison role between Falwell and my folks, he originally thought those efforts would help them out.) He was the one my dad had entrusted to look after his family while he was in prison. So I was thrilled. What could be better than flying out with Roe so we could both see my dad?

Roe took me to Minnesota on January 17, 1992, and dropped me off at the prison the next morning at eight. Having just turned sixteen, I was finally old enough to see my dad alone.

I filled out the required papers with the help of a cheat sheet Mom had prepared. Since my dyslexia always made me nervous about anything to do with writing, she had spelled out certain words she knew I'd need on a scrap of paper. That helped. Then I signed in for the first time and stored my stuff in a locker. It felt weird not having my mom or my sister there, but I was excited. I'd never gone by myself to see my dad. And now I would sit down with him, and he would help me out.

I crossed the tan-tiled visiting room and bought muffins, bagels, fruit, juice, and coffee from the vending machines. After microwaving the muffins and loading them up with butter, I settled in at one of the short tables that were perfect for putting up your feet, an act that always triggered a directive to lower your feet from the guards. Some of those guys were petty enough to do whatever they could just to dehumanize you. I laid everything out and waited, feeling very grown up.

"Wow, there he is!" I thought when my dad arrived ten minutes later. After a quick hug, we sat down, ate, and talked, just the two of us. We must have talked about everything—the birds and the bees, PTL, Suzanne, and how my heart was broken. Dad told me about his first love in high school and how he too had felt heartbroken. Then the conversation rolled around to that *Enquirer* article claiming that Mom and Roe were having an affair.

"What do you think?" Dad asked.

"Oh no, Dad, that's just a big joke," I answered.

"You're really sure, Son?"

"Dad, I'm a hundred percent sure," I said dismissively. "There's no way that Mom would lie to me, and Mom has already told me that it wasn't true. Besides, I would know. There's no way this is happening. Don't worry about it."

He believed me, and the conversation moved on.

Our eight hours together were over before I knew it.

"Dad, what a perfect day!" I exclaimed. "This has literally been the greatest day of my whole life."

I had spent my whole life trying to get my dad's attention, and finally I had had him all to myself for an entire day.

By the time Roe picked me up that afternoon, I was too exhausted from all my emotions to even think about really partying hard—my usual M.O. during these Minnesota visits. When dinner plans with some of my friends fell through, I asked Roe if he wanted to get a bite to eat. We headed down to the hotel restaurant, where I always got the same thing: a turkey dinner built to look like an ice-cream sundae, complete with a scoop of cranberries in place of the maraschino cherry on top.

We sat in a booth by a window on the far side of the restaurant, one of two that I always sat in with my mom. I couldn't get over what a great day I'd had with Dad.

"But you know, Dad asked me about the *Enquirer* article about Mom leaving him," I said. "It's funny. Dad thought it was true."

"I think it's true too," Roe said quietly.

"What?" I blurted.

"Well, your mother is planning on leaving your father," Roe said. "And if she leaves your father, I'm very interested in her."

I felt as if he had just taken a shotgun from underneath the table and blasted me. Shocked, I didn't know what to think.

"Roe, if you hurt my father, I will just kill you!" I threatened.

Then I got up from the table and left.

That night I lay in bed chain-smoking. Roe and I were sharing a room. Since he never smoked, I knew the smoke was probably driving him crazy, but I just didn't give a hoot. He was stealing my mother away from my father.

The nightmare just didn't end. PTL had been destroyed. My dad was in prison. I had lost my girlfriend. And on top of all those things crumbling around me, now my mother was leaving my father. The world as I knew it was going to completely change again, sending me back into another complete whirlwind. I just couldn't believe it.

As I lay in bed, I realized that in the morning I would have to get up and tell my dad that Mom was leaving him. That's when I started praying.

"Lord, please help me fall asleep," I said, jittery from the seven cups of coffee I had consumed that evening. "Please let me get a good sleep. I have to talk to my dad tomorrow."

I dozed off a few minutes later.

I awoke to the phone ringing. It was my mom.

"What's going on?" she asked.

Of course she knew, having already spoken to Roe on the phone the night before.

"Mom, you have one very angry young man on your hands," I sputtered.

"Are you going to tell your father?" she asked.

"You bet I am," I said.

I still couldn't believe it. And I couldn't believe that my mom, who was my best friend, had hidden this from me.

At the prison I had to stand in the same line and fill out the same forms. But this time, instead of feeling so independent and so much like a man, I felt like death. I was the distraught bearer of bad news.

I followed the guards through the sets of metal doors, past all the security checkpoints, and sat in the visiting room filled with dread.

Dad walked out excitedly, anticipating another awesome day. One look at me told him something was wrong. Yesterday's glow had been replaced with a mask of sorrow.

"What's wrong, Son?" he asked after we sat.

"Dad, promise me that you'll never leave me," I said, trying hard not to cry.

"What's wrong?" he repeated.

"Dad, promise me you'll never leave me," I insisted.

I didn't know how he would handle it. I knew how much my mom meant to him, and I was afraid maybe he'd kill himself or just give up and go crazy. And I just knew that I needed my dad there.

"I promise, I promise," he finally said.

So I told him.

"It's true," I said simply. "It's true, Dad."

"What's true, Son? What's true?"

"Mom is leaving you. And Roe told me he's interested."

All of a sudden, I was the one giving the shotgun blast. Dad's whole countenance dropped, and he slumped back into his chair as if shot. He sat in silence for two hours. He just couldn't believe it. And I couldn't either.

Finally I told him that I was going to leave home.

"Son, you don't need to leave," he said.

"I'm not gonna stay with Mom," I insisted. "I can't do it right now. I'm too devastated."

We didn't say much more, both of us caught up in our own misery. For my part, I couldn't help feeling that we had reached the end of the rope. I can only imagine what he was feeling.

After playing some cards to pass the time, the melancholy visit was finally up. I hugged my dad hard.

"I love you, Son. We'll work something out," he promised, before resignedly walking toward the room where they would perform the routine post-visitation body search to make sure that no drugs had been squirreled away in a body cavity.

As my dad returned to his cell to dwell on his wife's leaving him for another man—someone he considered a close friend at that—I had to travel back with Roe. It seemed that the credits were ready to roll on my family's life. I held him responsible.

Though I had little to no experience driving—and no permit of any kind—Roe had me drive to the airport two hours away. I felt as if I were with the enemy. Like Jerry Falwell before him, this was one more person who had come to destroy my family.

Before I pulled out of the parking garage, I pointed out to Roe that he had neglected to buckle up.

"Oh, that's all right, Son. I don't need to wear a seat belt," he answered.

"Don't you ever call me 'Son,'" I hissed.

I was in such a rage. For months I had harbored anger because my father was in prison, because we had lost PTL, because I felt as if the church hadn't been there for me, for us. I was angry with the world for making fun of a family being destroyed. Most of all, I was angry with myself. I kept thinking back to my dad's telling me that I had to be the man of the house. And I'd blown that off. And now Roe was messing with my family.

"I could just run this car off the road," I thought. "That would take care of him."

My mother picked us up from the airport. The fact that Roe drove back with us incensed me even more, and I refused to say a word to either. The moment I got home, I called Bo and asked him to pick me up. Then I packed the remainder of my clothes.

"I'm leaving," I told my mom bluntly. "How could you do this to Dad? He's in prison. How could you do this to him?"

When Bo arrived, I threw my luggage in the trunk of his car and climbed in. Then I started crying. Bo just grabbed me and hugged me.

"Man, I am so sorry, so sorry this is happening to you," he said.

"When is this all gonna end?" I muttered through my tears.

My mom called me that night at Bo's house. It didn't

help. By the time I got off the phone, I was screaming. In my fury, I knocked over a lamp.

"What's wrong?" Bo's mom, Carlene, asked as she ran up. "I thought somebody had died back here."

As usual, Carlene didn't let me be a baby and wallow in my own sadness. At the time, I just thought she was being insensitive. But in her own tough-love way, she really helped bolster my courage and my defenses. I'll always be grateful for that.

Over the next couple of weeks, my sister and my dad tried to talk me into returning home. I finally did, but with such a feeling of loss that even now my stomach hurts just thinking about it. I felt triply abandoned—by my dad, by Suzanne, *and* by my mom.

Though Bo and his family had reached out to me, I felt alone and hopeless. My life seemed wrecked beyond repair.

7

From Heritage to Hell

In a last-ditch effort to save the marriage,
Dad convinced Mom to go see a counselor in California. So
we flew out to Los Angeles and stayed at his cousin Marge's
house. The only things that came out of the three-week trip
were my first earring (my mother felt so guilty about everything that she agreed) and my getting kicked out of school.
Unfortunately, Mom had neglected to mention to the school
authorities that we would be away. So between that and all the
days I'd skipped, I came back to a letter from school saying
that I was no longer attending as of the next day.

When I went to say good-bye to my counselor and all my
teachers, most expressed their best wishes and left it at that.
My math teacher, Mrs. Berk, went a step further.

"I believe in you, Jay," she told me. "Even if you never return to school, I believe that you'll make it in this life and that you have something to offer in this world."

I don't know what she saw in me, but that kept me going for a long time.

Then my mom decided to move to California.

"Do you want to go?" she asked.

"I'd rather not," I said.

She didn't press the issue.

By early May 1992, all the furniture in our Florida house had either been crated or sold. Only my room remained intact. In another demonstration of deep denial, I had refused to pack up my belongings until the last possible day.

The night before I was to finally move everything out, I went over to the house after taking quite a few psychedelic mushrooms. Before I knew it, I was in the middle of a really horrible trip. I thought I was dying. All I wanted was for my mother to help me. But she had already left for California. The only way I could get through was to crawl in bed and pretend that she was in her room, that nothing in the house had changed, and that everything was fine.

In short, I was in hell again.

I stayed with Bo and his family that summer. That fall I went to stay with my dad's former secretary, Shirley Fulbright, who had offered to care for me in addition to continuing to run my parents' ministry with my sister's help.

I loved Shirley, a strong, classy blonde with a Georgian accent, who had been a member of our family's inner circle since I could remember. So staying with her brought back a semblance of normalcy. We made our own rules, like never talking in the mornings because we were both so grumpy. She quickly became my second mom.

In May, however, Shirley announced we were moving two hours away to St. Petersburg, Florida, where Bob D'Andrea, the owner of Channel 22, had offered to give us a condo to live in. So much for feeling comfortable! I didn't have a whole lot of friends in the new area, so I spent most of my time on our twelfth-floor balcony smoking cigarettes, looking at the ocean, and talking to friends in Orlando on the phone.

By that point, though I took a few outside classes, there was little to no talk about my officially returning to school. After so many failures, there just didn't seem like much point.

I ended up working as a cameraman for Channel 22, where every so often people who had been on my dad's television show or who I'd known from PTL would come through. Despite the job and the love Shirley showered on me, I was having trouble holding it together. Here I was—a high-school dropout with a drinking problem that I refused to acknowledge. Small wonder.

Then Shirley told me about a church's youth group I should check out. I got so excited, I went out and bought new tennis shoes like the Beastie Boys wore. By then I'd gotten my other ear pierced. I thought I was Mr. Cool. I couldn't wait to go.

The service was held at a little old house that had been gutted and repainted. About a hundred kids sat in the ten rows of metal chairs that faced a black stage. After a skit and twenty minutes of worship music, the youth pastor got up and went to take the offering.

"Don't worry," he said with a smile. "I'm not going to pull a Jim and Tammy Bakker on you and try to steal all your money."

I felt as if my heart had just been ripped out. Here I had decided to give God a chance. I thought maybe God was bringing me out to St. Pete to give me another chance to get to know Him. Then Mr. Hot Shot Youth Pastor makes a joke at my expense. That was my family—and my name—that he was belittling. Those were two people I loved with all my heart.

I lasted through the rest of the service, then walked up the little steps to the stage afterwards to wait for the pastor.

"I'm sorry, but I'm not comfortable with this," I told him as calmly as I could when we finally spoke. "That's my mom and dad you're talking about."

He never even apologized, which only reinforced my feeling that the church had completely rejected my family and turned its back on us. Another nail had been pounded in the coffin, reminding me that the church thought my family was worthless, and the world pretty much agreed. One more reason not to serve God.

I started sneaking beers up to the house and drinking in my room alone. Little did I know that things were about to get worse. A lot worse.

Around Christmas 1992, I was sitting in my room when I started to panic for no apparent reason. As the minutes ticked by, I felt more and more scared. I didn't really know what was wrong with me, but I remembered a friend telling me that he no longer smoked pot because it made him feel that he was going crazy. Now here I was, starting to feel as if I were losing my mind, and I hadn't even smoked anything.

I picked up the telephone and called my friend.

"Is this what you were talking about?" I asked.

"Yeah, but I don't like to talk about it because it freaks me out," he replied.

That's when I realized that he had been suffering from acid flashbacks, and now so was I.

"Just go take a warm shower, lie down, and try to relax," he advised. "That's all you can do."

So that's what I did. I took a warm shower, put on music, and tried to calm myself down. It helped a bit, but not much. And it did nothing to stave off other attacks in the days and weeks that followed. Everything around me would become unbearably bright. With my senses on total overload, I felt as if I were in another realm. The fear was absolute and unrelenting, making me feel as if I were going insane.

It got to the point where I couldn't even leave the house. We'd be out at a restaurant and I'd have to go home, too terrified and sick to remain in public. One time on the way to Bo's house, I had to have my friend who was driving pull over to the side of the road because I couldn't handle seeing the scenery speed by. Another time, I wound up sitting in a McDonald's for two hours because my panicked flashbacks were so bad that I couldn't get back into the car.

I could barely eat, and my eyes hurt all the time. Soon I couldn't handle being outside because the sun was so intense.

Life quickly boiled down to moments of sheer terror just strung together, one after the other. It got to the point where just leaving the house would trigger an acid flashback. I didn't know what to do. I thought about killing myself, but feared that hell would consist of a series of acid flashbacks that never went away.

Finally I flew out to visit my dad. The trip was a nightmare, with one panic attack following another in the plane and then in the hotel.

"Dad, I feel like I'm going crazy," I confessed when I saw him the next day. "I'm having acid flashbacks, and I'm scared of everything."

Just saying those words started to trigger a flashback right in the prison.

"If I have to get surgery where they take fluid out of my spine or cut a piece of my brain out, I'll do it. Whatever has to be done, Dad, I'll do it. Because I can't live in this terror anymore."

Dad sent me to see the same psychiatrist, Dr. Bazel Jackson, who had helped him during his trial. I stayed with him for two weeks, during which time he put me on Thorazine, which proved a miracle for me. The drug stopped the panic attacks and allowed me to get on with my life.

"One day, you're going to have to stop running," the psychiatrist told me when I left. "I don't know what you're running from, but you're running from something."

If he only knew how right he was! Not only was I running from the pain and hurt of being so alone, I was running from God because I had no idea of who He truly was.

8

The Prodigal Son

You would think that I might have gotten the message that I needed to slow down and take a good, hard look at myself and the choices I was making. I did the opposite. I headed straight for Orlando and resumed partying until I got to the point where I was wearing myself thin again. Instead of curbing my substance abuse, I simply switched gears. Since I couldn't do acid any longer and had been forced to give up pot almost completely since it triggered the acid flashbacks, I simply escalated my alcohol consumption. It got to the point where I was starting to black out every time I drank.

I knew this couldn't be good for me, but I didn't care. Drinking made me feel like a superhuman. All my insecurities and fears were just gone. My main goal was to build up my tolerance so I could drink even more.

The one thing that penetrated my alcoholic fog was my continued desire to get my dad released from prison.

On November 16, 1992, three years after my dad went to prison, I testified at a sentence-reduction hearing. After confessing that my embarrassing inability to spell (caused by my dyslexia) had kept me from writing letters to him in prison, I told the court that I needed my dad "more than anything I've ever needed in my whole entire life."

By all accounts, my testimony was instrumental in Dad's sentence being reduced from forty-five to eight years. For the first time, a human element had been injected into the proceedings. But eight years was still way too long.

I looked up to my dad so much. I know he's a human being, and the man made some mistakes, but he wasn't imprisoned for the mistakes he made. Even the IRS investigation into his business practices hadn't led to any charges. He was in prison because people disapproved of his lifestyle. And that wasn't a crime.

In truth, my dad was my ultimate role model. He showed me how to love people. I can remember him taking me to all sorts of ministry events when I was a kid and always showing me how important it was to serve others. I remember praying that God would take away all Dad's unbearable pain and give it to me instead. I just couldn't stand to see him depressed or going through any more hardships than he already had to confront. And I couldn't stand seeing him in prison.

Just a few weeks before, Dad had actually gotten out of prison for two days to see his father—my grandfather—who was in the hospital with internal injuries following a car accident on Christmas Day. Being with Dad in that little yellow hospital room, watching him trying to devour life by wolfing down the Big Mac, Kentucky Fried Chicken, and pizza I'd gotten him, reinforced my sense that I had to do whatever I could to get him out.

As the time neared for my dad to return to prison, I just couldn't stand it.

"Dad, I need you! I need you!" I bawled. "Please don't leave."

It was like losing him all over again. Only this time, I was trying to say everything I didn't get to say the first time he went away.

"I just need you, Dad," I cried. "I need you in my life. I can't make it without you."

He had to go.

As he walked out of the room and down the hospital corridor, escorted by a prison official, I grabbed my sister and sobbed.

By early in 1993, I had finally concluded that I just had to do whatever it took to get him released. So during a visit that was supposed to last just three days, I told Dad that I wanted to stay and help get him out of prison. He agreed.

"Wow, I'm going to help my dad," I thought to myself excitedly. "He doesn't belong in prison, and I can finally do something to help get him out." I was ecstatic.

Dad had just met with the parole board, and at the end of the meeting the chairman looked him in the eye and said, "We believe you are innocent." He was granted parole. But because Dad's was a high-profile case, the decision had to be ratified in Washington, D.C. When Dad's case got to D.C., the decision of the parole board was revoked. Now, there was only one more chance to appeal for parole.

Phil Shaw, a local pastor in Rochester, Minnesota, who had supported my dad from the moment he got there, was helping him get together a presentation for this hearing. This booklet was prepared for the political appointees who headed up the national parole committee. This booklet told the true story of what happened at PTL. The material would prove that my dad never defrauded anybody by showing his plans for all those buildings they accused him of never intending to build. Dad and Pastor Shaw wanted to get as many religious leaders—and other potentially influential public figures—as possible to lend their names to the effort.

For the rest of the summer, I called churches around the country asking them to help my dad. After a few days of hotel living, Pastor Shaw invited me to stay at his house. By this point I was so gun-shy around people, especially ministry people, that the whole idea made me real nervous. I knew the

Shaw family really loved us, but I had been so hurt. Still, I took a chance and moved into an extra room in their home. And suddenly I was part of a family again. I got along great with their thirteen-year-old daughter and their eleven-year-old son, whom I regularly kept up past his curfew playing video games.

I even started to attend services at Phil Shaw's church, where I began to rediscover my spirituality and God. One Sunday morning right after his sermon, I was on my feet to pray when I got a vision of Christ standing behind me. Leaning against the back of the chair in front of me, my eyes closed, I saw Him put His arms on my shoulders. It was as if He had appeared through the crowd to tell me that He loved me and that everything was going to work out.

Every day I would head over to an office the size of a closet in Phil Shaw's church and get on the phone to plead my dad's case. Whenever someone sounded receptive, Tammy Sue (who was helping long-distance) or I would send out the package Dad and Pastor Shaw had put together. The idea was to get people to write a personal letter requesting that my dad's sentence be shortened and to request in newsletters or on TV shows that their parishioners do the same.

I was my dad's last hope, and I knew it. The stakes couldn't have been higher.

A few of the smaller churches quickly agreed to help. But when I called luminaries like Paul and Jan Crouch of the TBN

Christian network, I got a very different reaction. Considering that my dad had been the original president of TBN, which had since grown to be the biggest Christian network in the world, I figured that the Crouches were bound to stand behind my dad. They wouldn't even take my call.

I was crushed. Here I was, a sixteen-year-old kid battling to get my dad out of prison. My folks were divorced and I was alone, sitting in the middle of Minnesota in the home of a pastor I'd basically just met, trying to do everything I could think of to get my dad released. And instead of helping or even sympathizing, they just gave me the runaround.

Even the people Dad had helped with money and free airtime turned their backs. The disappointment was almost more than I could bear.

I put a call through to Pat Robertson. Though Dad had been the creator and original host of Robertson's *700 Club*, Pat Robertson wouldn't take my call either. His cohost told me to send some booklets, and they'd see what they could do. As far as I know, they never did a thing on my father's behalf. I guess Robertson still resented Dad's refusal to endorse his presidential candidacy in 1988, even though Dad's decision was based on his belief that politics and religion shouldn't mix. Maybe Robertson was also worried about how people would react to having Dad affiliated in any way with his conservative right-wing coalition. Perhaps he just felt that God hadn't forgiven my dad.

I called Oral Roberts's ministry and ended up talking to Richard Roberts, his son.

"Would you please help my dad?" I begged. "Would you help my dad get out of prison? Could you ask your people on TV to write letters to lower his sentence?"

"No, I can't do it because I got too many things to worry about," Richard answered.

"You know what?" I countered heatedly. "Your problem is that your heart is in your wallet. You're too worried about your wallet."

I couldn't believe it! When Richard Roberts got a divorce, my dad put him on TV when nobody wanted anything to do with him.

"We love this man," he told millions of viewers. "We want to restore this man."

"Would you at least write a personal letter?" I asked.

He promised to think about it.

These were pastors my dad had worked with and been friends with. Yet they were more worried about their daily concerns than about the unconditional love of Christ. When Jesus died on the cross, it says in Colossians 1:19–22:

> Yet now, he has brought you back as his friend. He has done this through his death on the cross, his own human body. As a result, he has brought you into the very presence of God and you are whole and blameless as you stand before Him without a single fault.

But these megapastors weren't hearing it. They saw no restoration, and they had no compassion for Dad—or for me.

"How can these men call themselves ministers?" I railed. "How can these people truly be servants of Christ?"

It was just tearing me to shreds. Experience had taught me to expect the worst, but my heart had hoped to be surprised. It wasn't. They had met every one of my bitter expectations, and then some.

I began to work night and day. I even called Vice President Al Gore and got to his personal secretary. I don't know if the vice president ever did write a letter on my dad's behalf, but it sure seemed funny that I got closer to him than I did to most of those pastors.

I got to the point where I was dialing out of habit rather than hope. Then I called Pastor Jimmy Swaggart. Considering their history, which included Dad's taking Swaggart off the air because of the latter's incessant attacks on other ministers, it probably wasn't the smartest move.

"This is Jay Bakker," I announced to his secretary. "I've called for Jimmy Swaggart. I'd like to ask him to help my dad."

Within a second, Swaggart was on the phone with me.

"Pastor Swaggart," I said.

"Jamie Charles," he answered, surprising me by using my childhood name. "What can I do for you today?"

"My dad's got a sentence hearing coming up. Would you

write a letter to the parole board asking for my dad's sentence to be reduced?"

I fully expected him to say no. After all, he and my dad hadn't exactly seen eye to eye.

"Yes, I sure would."

I couldn't believe it. I figured I'd push my luck.

"There's one more thing I need to ask you to do."

"What is it?"

"Could you go on TV and ask people to write to get my dad's sentence reduced?" I asked.

"Well, Jamie, I've already recorded all our shows for this month," he answered slowly. "I don't know if I could do it."

"Pastor Swaggart, I desperately need your help," I begged. "No one else will help me. I've called all these major pastors on TV, and not one will help me with my dad."

Once again, I was ready to have my heart torn out, as it had been so many times in the prior weeks. And, finally, my expectations were not met.

"I will go back and rerecord the endings of the shows," he promised.

That week he sent me a tape.

"I got a call the other day from Jim Bakker's sixteen-year-old son, Jamie Charles, asking if I would help," he pronounced at the end of the show. "This is what we've got to do. We've got to help this man get out of prison."

Jimmy Swaggart supported my dad because he knew that he was just a man who had made a mistake and that we can't judge people for how they fare in their daily battles. His willingness to overlook their theological differences and even their past conflicts taught me a lot about restoration.

He was one of the few who showed me such kindness. The lack of Christian charity, faith, and brotherhood that so many of the others showed stands as an indictment against the church today. Instead of following Jesus' examples and teachings, they wiped our family history like a dirty smudge on a stained-glass window of the church. They acted as if we had never existed, and through their denials they pushed me farther and farther away from the church I so desperately needed.

Jimmy Swaggart's support was like a lifeline. But it couldn't override all those other refusals. They made me feel as if I were getting beaten up all over again. And they made me question the church's love and even God's.

"Maybe God doesn't think that I'm good enough," I started to tell myself. "Maybe we're not good enough."

PART THREE

Redemption

9

The Seeds of Salvation

Despite our efforts, which prompted over three thousand people to write to the parole commission, my dad's appeal was denied on July 29, 1993. Still, the calls must have made a difference, because something was finally changing. Earlier that month, Dad had called with the most surprising news.

"I'm being moved, and I don't know where," he said hurriedly. "I'll call you when I get there."

Usually when a high-profile prisoner like my dad is transferred, they put him on a private plane. Because of his reduced sentence he was eligible to fly on a commercial airline. Our lawyers even called and offered to pay for my dad's ticket, as well as that of the U.S. marshal who would have to accompany him. Instead, they sent him chained on a bus and plane tour the prisoners call "diesel therapy," with stops at some of the worst prisons in the country.

As the days turned to weeks, my sense of terror grew. I never knew where my dad was or where he would show up next. He'd call from the road when he could, trying to sound encouraging. I wasn't fooled.

After twenty-one days of grueling travel, he ended up in Jesup, Georgia, a minimum-security facility work camp just three hundred miles from Heritage USA, where my grandparents still lived. Jesup, with its picnic benches in the yard, was a lot more pleasant. It was still prison, with cells and guards, but unlike the facility in Minnesota, it wasn't surrounded by a barbed-wire fence. Of course, visitors still had to go through all the same security procedures as before, and inmates still couldn't leave.

By then I had moved yet again, this time to Atlanta to live with Pastor Don Paulk and his family. Though I had only met them briefly once before, Bishop Earl Paulk and his brother, Pastor Don Paulk—who had marched with Martin Luther King Jr. for civil rights in the 1960s and founded one of Atlanta's truly integrated churches—and Don's wife, Clariece—an awesome pianist—had all been on Dad's show. When Dad first went to prison, they immediately offered to help with whatever was needed, including housing and educating Tammy Sue and me. With Dad's transfer to Jesup, that offer suddenly made a lot of sense. Besides, having me return to school was important to my dad.

I dreaded the whole idea.

Though my time with Pastor Shaw and his family had been like a reprieve, I didn't want to live in another pastor's house. I didn't want to go back to school. I didn't really want to quit my cameraman job in St. Pete, to which I had returned after my six-week stint in Minnesota. I didn't want to leave my friends. And I sure didn't want to give up drinking.

Still, I agreed to meet them. After all, living with them meant that I'd only be a hundred miles from my dad. The first night I was there, we were all sitting around the table in their Victorian-style dining room when *A Current Affair* came on. Suddenly there was Don Paulk on the TV screen waving off *Hard Copy* and *A Current Affair* reporters who were questioning him about an alleged affair he'd had, while his twenty-one-year-old son, Donnie Earl, tried to get him to just go inside the house.

It struck a chord in me. I remembered all those evenings our family had sat around the TV, wondering what the media was going to accuse us of next. I knew what they were feeling. It was as if I could think their very thoughts.

"This is where I'm supposed to be," I thought to myself.

Instead of holding what had happened to my family against me, they would understand what it was like to be rejected and judged. They would be able to understand me, because they were going through the same thing.

So I went back to St. Pete and packed up all my stuff. Saying good-bye to Shirley almost crushed me. I could not bear to leave her because she had shown me so much love. We were like this team going through hell together. But I had to go.

The decision to move to Atlanta and stay with the Paulks probably saved my life. But relief wouldn't come right away.

My parents' divorce had been finalized on March 13, 1992. A few months later, I received a letter from my mom explaining that she and Roe were getting married on October 3, 1993. "You're more than welcome to come, but I don't expect you to," she wrote. "I understand."

I'd felt shell-shocked ever since my parents' marriage had blown up. This just added a stamp of finality. Our family was fragmented, and there would be no getting back together. All hope was gone.

I was miserable.

Though I had finally slimmed down from the chunky Jamie Charles I'd been as a kid, I started regaining a lot of that weight, eating blueberry cobblers and Clariece's Southern cooking to make myself feel better. Soon I'd gained twenty pounds. I hated that.

My new school at the Paulk's church required me to put on a uniform and take my earrings out every morning. That was just the start of my trouble there. Despite my long absence from school, I was enrolled in all these crazy accelerated classes, and I wasn't very accelerated. I didn't do well, and I hated that. So half the time I just slept through the day instead.

I didn't hit it off right away with the Paulks' son, Donnie Earl—a good-looking jock, who had played college basketball—either. Despite a great first meeting, it wasn't until we went night fishing together a month or two later that we initiated the friendship that would soon bond us like brothers.

A few other bright moments crept into this dark time. I started going to church again, the only ironclad house rule, and in some small ways began to heal. One Sunday, Bishop Earl Paulk, Donnie's uncle, who headed the ministry, looked over to the congregation.

"Is there any youth here who feels like they want to be in ministry? That you want to spend your life serving God?"

No one moved. Then I got up and walked to the front. I didn't even realize that my action prompted others to join me.

"When I saw those kids following you, God showed me that you would work with young people and help change their lives," the Bishop later told me.

I was pleased that he had faith in me, because I sure didn't have faith in myself. Though I was now volunteering with the church's youth ministry, I still had little to no sense of self. I did what I could to straighten myself out while at the Paulks, but I hurt too much. The Paulks never gave me a hard time about my drinking or about the cigarettes I smoked in the backyard outside their home.

Donnie Earl's father, Don, who became like a second dad during that time, could see that I was suffering.

"Jay, I think you need to see a counselor," he said. By then I knew I needed help, so I didn't protest.

Don sent me to Jackie Thompson, a ruddy, thickset therapist with a rough past and a gentle manner, who was now affiliated with Paulk's church.

"Your family's ministry has helped me so much in the past, I won't charge you," Jackie said the first time we met. That meant a lot to me. I was angry about so many things, and he helped me bring up all the issues that were eating my insides. In time, I began to get my head straight and come out of my misery.

I continued to work on trying to get my dad out of prison. Every week I'd call his lawyer, Jim Toms, to get an update. Of course, he would always give me that whole "month or two" thing, which drove me nuts. Then one day, he mentioned in passing that Dad was going to meet with Jerry Falwell. I freaked out.

"There's no way this is going to happen!" I exclaimed.

"Oh, no. It's going to be fantastic," Toms argued.

I hung up the phone and called Shirley to ask if she knew anything about it.

"This can't happen!" I reasserted, with rising fury.

No one seemed to share my sense of urgency. This was the man who destroyed my father, who took everything we had, who destroyed my life. To me, he was an enemy not to be trusted. Would he use the visit to manipulate people into thinking he was a good man at my father's renewed expense? Was he going to make sure my dad would never be successful again? Or would he orchestrate a scenario that would literally kill my dad instead of just his reputation? I knew the power he held and what he was capable of. I'd seen how he lied, manipulated, and eventually destroyed my family. My parents were divorced, our lives had fallen apart, everything we knew was gone, and it all led right back to this man, Jerry Falwell.

Determined to prevent the inevitable betrayal I foresaw, I convinced Donnie Earl to take me down to see Dad that weekend.

"You can't meet with Falwell. You can't do this!" I insisted, my voice tight with fear, the tears rolling down my face.

By way of reply, my dad started to tell me about the importance of forgiveness—especially of one's enemies. As my hatred of the men who had turned on my dad had grown, he had been figuring out how to pray for them. This was my first glimpse of grace.

Yet even after he read me passages from a book titled *God Meant It for Good,* which he'd brought out to the visiting room with him, the idea of his meeting with Falwell still terrified me.

"He's coming to kill you," I said, crying, positive that this was just another trick to destroy my dad so he would never be a threat again. "He didn't kill you all the way the first time. Now he's coming to finish the job."

"I'll make a deal with you," Dad said. "*You* go meet with Falwell and talk with him. If you think I should meet with him, I will. If you don't, I won't."

It was as if he were saying, "You're the man, now; you're the head of the family. You go tell me what's safe. You look out for me." That my dad trusted me that much made me feel amazing.

Jim Toms refused to go along with the decision.

"I am not going to play these games!" he said angrily.

By that point, I was pretty fed up and angry with Jim Toms.

"I'm tired of you always telling me my dad's going to get out of prison," I lashed back. "My dad's still sitting in prison, and you haven't done anything for him."

When I told my dad about our conversation the next day, he backed me completely.

"Listen, you do what my son says, or you're not my lawyer anymore," he told Toms. "This is the way it's going to be done, period. You don't question my son."

It was decided that Jim Toms and I would fly down to Florida and go to this huge conservative Baptist church where Falwell would be speaking. The service began with a sermon about prisoners and young criminals deserving longer sentences. Having just listened to my incarcerated dad preach forgiveness, it all sounded like hate to me. I felt as if I were in the enemy's camp.

They had seated us right in front of Jerry Falwell. Years of anger and pain welled up inside of me at the sight of him.

"Jerry Falwell—the man who had shattered my father and his ministry—is right within range," I thought to myself. "I could just reach out and punch him, or wrap my fingers around his throat and squeeze."

The thoughts weren't exactly Christlike, and they certainly didn't reflect the lesson about forgiveness that my dad had just shared with me. That's something I still have to work on. But I was seventeen and angry at the world in general and Jerry Falwell in particular.

The service seemed to go on forever. They even brought up a couple of kids who gave their testimony about Falwell's impact on their lives. He had overhauled my life too.

Finally, we confirmed that we would meet with Falwell after a dinner he already had scheduled. So we headed back to the hotel, grabbed a bite to eat, and returned to our rooms to wait. At nine o'clock, they called to say they'd be a little late. An hour and a half later, they delayed again. Finally at midnight, they called and said they wouldn't be able to meet us until the next morning.

"It's a conspiracy," I thought. "They'll only give me five minutes in the morning and force a hasty decision."

We hadn't finished eating breakfast, when Falwell called down to say he was ready.

"Bring your breakfast up here," he offered, when told that we were in the middle of our meal.

Grabbing our Danishes and orange juice, we headed up to his room.

Upon our arrival, Falwell, looking as usual as if he'd been born in the suit he was wearing, stood up from the edge of the bed upon which he was seated and shook my hand.

"Hi. How are you?" he asked. "Nice to meet you."

"Hello," I said, pointedly leaving out anything about being pleased to meet him, since I wasn't.

After a short prayer, we all sat down at a table. Jim Toms explained that I had some concerns about the proposed meeting with my dad.

"You're a life changer," I said bluntly. "I look out the window every day, and I don't see the home I grew up in. When I go outside of my room, I don't see my mom and my dad. I don't see the life that I had. I watched my dad have a nervous breakdown. I watched my father go to prison. I sat with my father and had to tell him my mom was divorcing him."

For the next forty-five minutes, I pretty much blamed everything that had gone wrong in our lives on him.

"You called my dad a homosexual on TV! You know you

can't deny it, Jerry, because I saw you do it. I've got it on video. If you'd like to see it, I can send you a copy."

"Well, Jay, there's just certain things you don't understand," he countered repeatedly.

"All you wanted was the PTL Satellite Television Network," I continued. "You lied to us. You came to destroy us."

I explained in detail everything I had gone through, including the drinking and the drugs. I no longer cared if he knew. He couldn't hurt *me* much worse than he already had.

"Jay, you don't understand," he continued to say.

I'm not sure why, but suddenly I realized that Dad was right—this was about forgiveness.

"I just want to let you know that I forgive you," I said. "I forgive you for what you've done to my family, and I want you to forgive me for hating you all these years, for the hate that has lived in my life."

"Thank you for forgiving me," he replied. "Forgive me for what you may think I have done or might have done to you."

That conversation gave me peace in my heart for the first time in years. He did not say what I wanted to hear, but forgiving him was freeing.

"You *are* a life changer," I said, though even now I wonder if he realizes how wrong his actions were. "You've changed my life again. You've set me free, because I don't have to carry this hate in my heart anymore."

I felt as if a freaking dead man had been taken off my back. Through my hate and rage, I'd been carrying Falwell around with me all these years. By forgiving him, I put him behind me.

Jim Toms and I went into the adjoining room to confer.

"Yeah, let's let them meet," I agreed.

I didn't want to deny my dad the euphoria of freedom that forgiveness had triggered. It felt better than any drug I had ever taken.

We got on Falwell's private jet to fly down to meet with my dad. Their meeting still scared me, but I knew it wasn't about Jerry Falwell anymore. It was about forgiving and moving on with our lives.

Besides, I would be there with my dad every step of the way. So I thought.

"You can't come back here," the warden announced to me when we got to the prison. "You have to wait outside."

The alarm inside my head sounded louder than any prison alarm could have.

"Wait a second. This is part of the deal," I argued angrily. "This is the whole reason we brought Jerry Falwell down here."

The warden, a great fan of Falwell's, refused to relent. My sense of panic mounted.

What if Falwell was still scamming and planning to hurt my dad again? Now Dad wouldn't have me to defend him. But I had no choice. I had to trust God.

They met for close to two hours. When the visit was over, they let my dad come to the front door of the prison. At the sight of each other, we both just glowed, like two kids who have just discovered life.

"You look as if a million pounds has been taken off your shoulders," my dad said.

He looked just as relieved and just as excited. Once again, the power of forgiveness had done its work.

Though Jesus died on the cross to forgive us for our sins, for some reason we Christians have a hard time forgiving one another. Yet after five years in prison, my father had given me my first taste of who Jesus really was.

10

Praying on the Outside

Though I didn't know it, I had learned a lesson about grace. But I would have more to learn about applying it to my own life.

Against the advice of Don Paulk, I decided to leave their home in Atlanta and return to Florida to live with Bo for the summer. The second I got down to Florida, I went on a drinking spree for two or three days. That was just the start of the insanity. I partied that whole summer, spending up to four hundred dollars a week at the bars and clubs I frequented nightly.

I had made a deal with Carlene, Bo's mom, that I would work on getting my GED by attending night classes. I lived up to the letter, rather than the spirit, of the agreement. As soon as class let out, instead of returning home to do home-work or study, I partied.

Still, I didn't think I was an alcoholic. All my friends drank as much as I did, so I figured nothing was wrong.

"Besides, I can stop drinking anytime," I reasoned. "I even lasted an entire week without a drink."

Of course, I had still gone to all the clubs during my temporary sobriety. And as soon as I had proved to myself that I didn't have a drinking problem, I went right back to getting drunk.

Though the establishments would mark my hand to show that I was under twenty-one, I'd wash the stamp off the second I got in. Since they gave out wristbands to anyone of age, I'd find one that someone had torn off and use chewing gum to stick it back together on my arm. Then I'd get wasted and dance all night.

That July (1994), I got the totally shocking news that Dad was being released. Finally! I couldn't believe it. I immediately started making plans to join him.

"You haven't upheld your end of the bargain," Carlene told me. "You were supposed to get your GED."

"I'm sorry. I can't stay," I replied. "I've waited for this for five years—my dad's getting out of prison!"

In an effort to dodge as much of the press as possible, they released Dad at three o'clock in the morning, which added to the sense of unreality. I drove to the Savannah airport to meet him. When I saw him, I just wrapped my arms around him.

"This isn't happening," I thought to myself.

He'd been gone so long and I was so numb from his absence that the whole thing just didn't seem real. I was in shock, plain and simple.

"This is crazy! Dad is out! I'm looking at him outside of a prison. This can't be reality!"

I called the Paulks from the airport.

"Dad's out of prison," I gloated. "He's right here with me."

I was so excited! This was everything I'd been waiting for. I had been thirteen when my dad was last a free man, and here I was eighteen. All those years—those formative years—without him.

We flew to Charlotte and then drove to the halfway house in Asheville, North Carolina, where my dad had to stay. They fingerprinted him when they checked him in. He knew just what to do, following orders without even blinking. It was like watching a pro.

"Are you happy to be here?" the press asked him.

"I'm happy to be anywhere," he said.

The next morning, we headed up to this small, strangely put together cabin in the mountains that Franklin Graham, Billy Graham's son, was renting for us. Tammy Sue, her husband Doug, and my nephews James and Johnathan, greeted us with a WELCOME HOME DAD, WE LOVE YOU!!! sign they had made. Then we sat, ate, and talked until it was time for him to return to the halfway house for the night.

From then on, Dad spent as little time as he could in the halfway house. Every weekday, he would leave there at the crack of dawn and return late at night. On weekends, he could just stay in the cabin with me.

I finally had my dad back. It should have been great.

It wasn't.

Even though Don Paulk had warned me about putting all my eggs in one basket, I guess part of me had subconsciously expected that things would be just like they were before Dad had gone to prison, if not better. But life had changed.

For starters, Mom wasn't there. Her absence was so loud, it was ridiculous. You could feel it in every room.

I had assumed that Dad and I would be best friends and spend all our time hanging out together. But after such a long separation, we didn't know how to react to each other. I wanted to be with him, but I also wanted to continue seeing friends he didn't think I should hang out with. For five years I'd been functioning fairly independently. Suddenly, Dad was telling me how to live my life.

Of course, my alcoholism helped erect a wall between us too.

"If you don't come home right now, I'll never give you another dime," he threatened once when I was partying in Charlotte (which I did every weekend and sometimes into the week that followed). "I'll never support you. You'll be cut off completely."

"You're just like your mother," he yelled another time, when I opted to stay in Atlanta instead of flying somewhere with him. "You just want to have a good time."

His disapproval was hard to take. The escalating conflict between us became worse. Our fights tore me to shreds.

"Shut up!" I screamed one afternoon after he kept telling me how to drive.

I know that made him really angry, but it felt as if nothing I did was good enough. What I wanted most was for him to acknowledge all the work I had done on his behalf while he was in prison. He never did. Instead, he doled out the same kind of tough love his father had given him. That was not what I needed.

Soon after, Dad heard about a program in Phoenix, Arizona, called Master's Commission, which is basically a boot camp for kids who want to get started in the ministry. Master's Commission teaches them how to do short-term missions or outreaches by going out on the streets to entertain kids with skits and lip-synching to Christian songs, then talking with them about God, and trying to win them to Jesus.

"Listen, Son, if you fly out there and try it and don't like it, you can come back here and live however you want," Dad promised. "Just go out and give it a shot."

Feeling that despite all I'd done for him, I'd proved a disappointment to my father, I agreed to go. I'd always wanted to be a pastor, because I always had a heart for people and longed to help them. From the time I was a little boy, I'd felt a call to serve God. This could get me started.

Aware of how strict the organization was, I smoked my last cigarette on my way there, savoring every drag.

As it turns out, the kids at Master's Commission had been warned about me even before I got there.

"Jay Bakker's coming, and he's the worst of the worst," the Master's Commission director told them.

Once again, I had been branded a sinner and an alcoholic. Whether either one or both was true, I was basically just a hurting kid whose life had been torn to shreds. With Dad finally out of prison, I had no purpose anymore and nothing to fight for. Worse, my dreams of how right everything would be once he was set free had been shredded as well.

As soon as I arrived in Phoenix, I was notified that in addition to a no-smoking and no-drinking policy, Master's Commission had a no-dating rule as well.

"Well, Dad certainly forgot to tell me about *this* one," I thought.

Then five kids, one of whom they'd actually flown in from Los Angeles since I'd gone to school with her at Heritage USA, took me out to eat. As I later found out, each had been assigned a different role. "You play the mean guy, and you try to be the tough older brother, and see how he responds to you," they were told. The girl I knew was to be the person who was real open to me.

Since I didn't know any of that at the time, our interaction proved a little overwhelming. Still, everyone seemed nice enough. That night, they showed me the apartment I'd be sharing with two of the best students at Master's Commission. The room I stayed in was decorated with life-size posters of contemporary Christian musicians who I considered cheesy. I never even listened to Christian bands.

"What am I doing here?" I wondered.

I got my answer when I started to talk to Kelli Miller, a short hippie with long brown hair who, in her mismatched disco shirt and patched corduroys, looked as if she'd stepped out of the 1970s.

Naturally we talked about doing ministry, something I'd been thinking more and more about ever since working with Donnie Earl's youth ministry.

"I want to reach out to the punk rockers and skateboarders like the ones in Atlanta," I said. "I even talked to my friend Donnie Earl about opening a coffeehouse where punk-rock kids and skateboarders could hang out and have someone to talk to twenty-four hours a day. I just want to be able to be there for people who are struggling and going through hard times. To really love them."

Kelli was blown away.

"No way!" she cried. "That's really weird, because me and this guy Mike Wall are starting a ministry like that called Revolution. As a matter of fact, we had this one outreach with punk bands, and it was really cool."

"I'd really love to be a part of that," I exclaimed.

I spent the next three days trying hard to adjust to the guys in Master's Commission. In tried-and-true fashion, I even tried to dress like them. It didn't work. Not only did I feel out of place, this just wasn't where I wanted to be. All these guys were focused on living and acting the way Christians are supposed to act, talking the way Christians are supposed to talk, and listening to the music that Christians are supposed to listen to. It was like living in another country or another world.

In the mornings, we'd get up and go to the Phoenix First Assembly. With all the lights off, we'd pray for an hour. I don't think I ever remembered praying for an hour in my life before. On the third morning, I prayed with all my heart.

"Lord, if You want me, if You need me, You got me. Just give me an answer. Show me what to do. I'm here for You. I just need to know what You got planned for me. Just take me, Lord. Just use me; I'm Yours. Here's Your chance."

The next afternoon, I met Mike Wall.

"Hey man, you want to go skateboarding?" he asked when he called.

I didn't have my board with me, but Mike was talking my language!

"I'm on my way over," he announced. "We'll go get a bite to eat."

When Mike arrived at my apartment with his friend, Ryan, they intimidated the hell out of me. Both looked like oversized skinheads. Jeans, combat boots, and band shirts added to their tough look.

"These guys are hard-core," I thought. "What's that all about?"

I found out over lunch. And then dinner. Mike told me all about the plans for Revolution, which including having punk and hard-core bands play before every service.

"Let's just do it," I cried. "Let me help you start Revolution. I want to be a part of it."

Mike was excited.

Even though he had spent four years in Master's Commission and Kelli had spent two years there, you weren't allowed to be on staff with Revolution if you were in Master's Commission. So the next day I sat down with Lloyd Zigler, the head of Master's Commission.

"You know, I really feel as if God's calling me to do this ministry with Mike and Kelli," I told him. "I want to help them start this ministry."

"Okay, I respect that. God's call on your life," he replied.

Then he released me.

I really appreciated his recognizing that I'd found my special purpose, though I'm sure he didn't mind having one less kid to worry about, especially a heavy drinker with my reputation.

Leaving Master's Commission also meant leaving my housing behind. Though newly married, Mike and Heather opened their home to me and included me in their lives. During that time, Mike, who reminded me in ways of Donnie Earl, and I had grown close. Though he really functioned as my leader and pastor at the time, he was also like my big brother. Friendships like that don't come along very often. We went to the movies and to shows, slam-danced together, and stayed up all night playing Nintendo. We also prayed together, poured over scriptures in the Bible, which up until that point I'd actually never really read, and spent hours in deep conversation. It was as if God were preparing us for what we were about to launch.

It would take six months of strategizing, training, staff meetings, and getting to know local kids before we could really get started. The time I spent reading the Bible and praying alone, sometimes for two hours a day, changed my life. Somewhere along the way, God became real to me, despite continued attacks by some of the church on my family.

"Don't become prideful, because pride will make you fail. Look at what happened to Swaggart [who had recently

The day my dad was released from prison. It seemed as though I had waited my entire life for that moment.

(Above) Mom, Tammy Sue, and me at Amanda's and my wedding shower. This was the first time in eight years that I had seen my mom and dad together.

(Right) Donnie Earl Paulk and his wife, Brandy, with their new little girl, Esther.

(Opposite) The original Revolution staff, looking pretty cheesy on our one-year anniversary. From left to right: Regina Parnum, Heather Wall, Kelli Miller, Mike Wall, and me.

Hanging out with my friend and tattoo artist Ryan Weaver, with Jerry Only from the Misfits.

In April 2000 I took the Revolution staff to visit the abandoned Heritage USA. Just seeing it again brought back all the bad memories, but it also made me realize how far I had come since then. I left that day with a whole new perspective on life.

(*Above*) For Larry King's fifteenth-anniversary show in May 2000, he wanted the whole Bakker family. It was the first time we had been on TV together in eleven years.

(*Right*) My parents as newlyweds . . .

(*Opposite*) . . . and the happiest day of my life, my marriage to Amanda.

Amanda and me, starting our new life together.

been exposed for moral failures] and Bakker," advised one of Mike Wall's favorite preachers in Phoenix during a Sunday service.

The deep wound in my heart had been stabbed again. I knew that this wasn't God talking. I still feel that God chose my father and our family to go through our ordeal because we were strong enough to withstand it. But that didn't mean that it didn't hurt.

"Why is that man saying this about my father?" I asked myself in anguish.

Even my pain was a source of conflict, since people around me had started making me feel bad for feeling bad.

"Get over it," they advised. "Roll with the punches."

But I wasn't able to let those comments roll off my back, and that made me feel even worse. Torn up, I didn't hear another word of the sermon.

Going to church, the one place that should have provided solace, became an unending round of Russian roulette, but with all five bullets in the chamber. The disenchantment fueled my desire to do Revolution even more.

For our big debut, Mike booked a band called Scapegoat, and my dad donated the whole sound system for Revolution from his old church as well as a bunch of metal chairs. We put up a simple flyer that just said "Revolution, Sunday Night." To our amazement, over a hundred kids showed up.

Mike started preaching as only he could. His theatrics included smashing a TV with a sledgehammer. Later he would blow up a lightbulb in a microwave. One time he asked me to pretend I was throwing up on stage. What we were doing was so controversial that youth groups, even the one from the church that sponsored Revolution, were banned from coming. But the kids loved all the stuff we did. Before long, we had kind of become rock stars with a message from God. We were pioneering something new. No one in Phoenix had seen anything like this.

We made a great team, since I wanted to work with skateboarders, Mike was into punk rockers, and Kelli related to hippies. Before we knew it, we had grown into this really big ministry. Revolution was even asked to be the premier ministry at Pastor School, a yearly event attended by thousands of pastors who come to check out what different ministries across the country are doing. In addition, Tommy Barnett, the pastor at Phoenix First Assembly, asked me to give my testimony.

"I wonder if you'd be interested in calling your dad to see if he'd come up for it," he added.

Though Dad said it didn't look as if he could come, that was no big deal to me. Everything else was finally working.

Never having spoken publicly before, I was really nervous about sharing the intimate details of my life with thousands. Up to this point, I had just been doing sound at Revolution and working one-on-one with the skaters, so most of the kids didn't even know who I was. That only added to my apprehension.

I would be on stage with some fifty young punks, skaters, and hippies from Revolution. When it was time for us to go out, a really cool video that Mike's friends had made about us cranked up. These bells started ringing—bong, bong, bong—followed by rattling that sounded just like an earthquake. Then it cranked into this punk song by MXPX called "Bad Hair Day." All the while, the video showed the skateboarders, punk rockers, and other kids who made up Revolution. It was awesome!

After Mike shared the vision of Revolution, Pastor Tommy came out on stage.

"I want some of your kids to give their testimonies," he said.

That's when they called me out.

I walked away from the Revolution crowd on stage, toward the seven thousand members of the audience. When I reached the microphone, I started talking about the great ministry we'd started. But that wasn't what Pastor Tommy wanted to hear.

"Tell them who you are," he said in a low voice. "Tell the people your name. Tell them who your parents are."

Once again, this wasn't about me—this was to be about Mom and Dad. But that was okay. I was very proud of them.

"I'm Jay Bakker. Jim Bakker is my dad. Jim and Tammy Faye Bakker are my parents," I said.

The crowd of thousands of pastors went crazy, rising to their feet as they applauded. Their acclaim felt a little odd. Here I was in an Assemblies of God church, the same Assemblies of God that had defrocked my father and wanted nothing to do with him just a few years earlier. I was sure that half the people in that church had preached against my dad in the late 1980s. But all of a sudden they were excited to see me.

"We love you, Jamie Charles," they yelled out.

Since I had introduced myself as Jay, I knew these had to be people who grew up watching—and loving—my family. I started to bawl right there on stage. After seven years of being held up to condemnation and ridicule, my family was finally being accepted again.

"You don't know how much that means to me," I managed to say through my sobs.

It took me a while to recover. The crowd got quiet. Then someone screamed out, "We love you." That almost set me off again.

Despite all the recent reading I'd been doing, I didn't know a lot of the Bible. All I knew was religion and what religion had done to me. So I just preached my guts and my heart out and told them the truth about how we should act as Christians.

"We've got to start loving each other and stop judging and destroying one another," I concluded, referring to Matthew 7:1–3, along with Mark 12:31, which commands us to love our neighbor as ourselves. "My family used to say you can make it by faith. Now we say you can make it from experience."

Once again, the audience went nuts.

"Jay, we've got a surprise for you," Pastor Tommy announced when I'd finished.

Then he introduced my dad.

It had been almost a decade since my father had stood up in front of a church crowd and preached. As he walked forward, the crowd stood to their feet applauding for at least five minutes.

"I'm scared," he whispered to me when he got to the stage.

"So am I," I replied.

Before we left, we talked to Tommy Barnett about keeping the tape confidential. Every year they sell the Pastor School tape, but this year they promised they wouldn't release it to the press or anyone else. That agreement lasted just until *Charisma* magazine decided they wanted to air it on their TV show. That's how things seem to work out so often in Gospel Hollywood.

"This is such an awesome, personal thing that happened to you guys that we're not going to do anything with it," they promised.

Then a few weeks later, it was released to every TV show and magazine in America. Another private Bakker moment shared with the world.

The church was starting to come around, but they hadn't gotten it completely. It was still reconciliation on their terms.

11

Lost and Found

Before I knew it, a year had passed since my coming to Phoenix. Everything seemed to be going right. I spent my days making up fliers to promote upcoming Revolution events, putting together professional skateboarding and punk music shows, raising money by selling Revolution T-shirts I'd gotten silk-screened, and even getting a skateboarding half-pipe donated to the ministry. The goal was to provide kids with activities they liked in an arena where Jesus' message was delivered as well. And it worked. By now some seventy kids regularly attended all our functions. Our concerts drew hundreds more.

Despite our successes with Revolution, however, strains were developing. Though Mike kept telling me that if he were ever going to have an assistant pastor it would be me, I felt that my role was becoming less and less prominent, as he brought in other people and put them on staff.

Of course, I was still fighting my old demons as well. I still felt a lot of pain about my dad. I was also really trying to quit drinking at that point. I used skateboarding, movies, and religion to fill the void I'd previously filled with drugs and alcohol. But my addictions were doing pushups on the sideline, just waiting for me to slip. And I did. Every time I'd go to North Carolina, I'd start with nonalcoholic beers for the first couple of days and then wind up drinking and partying as usual. I'd return feeling guilty, sure that God hated me.

"What is wrong with me?" I wondered.

Since I was already beating myself up quite thoroughly, I didn't need anyone else to help on that front. Though Mike was only trying to make sure that I didn't fail again, he cast himself as the voice of judgment. Why was I going out to coffeehouses when I knew there were girls there, people dancing, and beers being served? Why was I just hanging out and talking with all the skateboarders? Was that really ministry?

Though both those latter activities involved some of the heaviest ministry I've ever done, Mike was always on my case. I'm sure he thought he was looking out for me. After all, I had made some pretty poor choices, and he knew it. But he was controlling every aspect of my life. He even weighed in on whom I should date. Of course, I allowed him to dictate what I should do. I was trying to stop sinning. It got to the point, however, where I was afraid to go out with the kids, because I was afraid they would see me as a human being.

The scrutiny—and the fear it triggered—wore on me.

"You've been at that coffee shop again, haven't you?" he asked accusingly one night.

Here I'd partied my whole life, in bars no less, and suddenly Mike didn't want me to go to a coffeehouse where they spun records because he was afraid I would lust after girls, which wasn't even the case.

Of course it was futile to argue, because if I disagreed with Mike, we would stay up all night discussing the issue. It got to a point where our friendship started to fade. The strain of the three of us living together during what was essentially Mike and Heather's honeymoon year didn't help.

Unable to take the tension anymore, I started to look for a place to live with my good friend Chris Gilbert, who had helped me with the skating ministry from the moment we'd met at the skate shop he worked in. With Chris's help, I also got a job at Little Caesar's Pizza just so I could have time away from the ministry.

"I've never felt so guilty in my life," I confessed to my mom when she came into town for a visit. I felt as if I could never be good enough, never live up to the expectations that had been foisted upon me.

One evening as I was doing sound for a guest speaker at Revolution, I just broke down for no apparent reason. After the service, I went skateboarding for a couple of hours to clear my head. Phoenix gets so hot that we often skateboarded during the cooler midnight hours.

When I finally got home at two in the morning, all the lights were off. Still, I noticed a note lying on the kitchen table.

"Jay, your dad called. Dr. Baiquiera died," the note read. "You grew up with his son. You need to fly out."

"Who?" I thought, puzzled.

All of a sudden, it registered.

"Oh my God. Blair Bycura died," I thought in horror. Our favorite neighbor at Tega Cay, one of Dad's best friends, and the father of my childhood pals was gone. I felt the tears well up.

"God, these people don't give a hoot about me," I thought, my perspective skewed by the grief that overwhelmed.

I wish they would have listened for me to come in and said, 'Hey, Jay, let's sit down. I've got something to tell you.'"

Instead, they had just left a sloppily written, misspelled note. The Bycuras were like family. Leaving that note was like saying that my whole life wasn't worth a thing.

"I can't live this life anymore," I thought. "If this is Christianity, if this is God, I can't live this way." This was the straw that broke the camel's back.

That night I called my dad, who confirmed that Blair had died in a plane crash, having suffered a heart attack while piloting a small aircraft. Dad was going to do the funeral.

"We need to be there for the Bycuras," he said.

"Of course we do," I replied.

We had lived the majority of our life in tragedy; now it was our turn to help them while they were going through their sorrow.

I flew down to Charlotte the next day, September 23, 1995. When I got there, Darren came out of the house to greet me.

"They had to use dental records to identify Dad," he told me.

Then he started to sob. I just grabbed him and held him. I hated seeing him and his brother going through such pain. But when they told me they wanted to go out and drink to get over things, I reacted like a pompous ass.

"You know, I don't drink," I told them. I knew if I drank God would be upset with me, or Mike Wall would find out, or God would tell Mike Wall, and I couldn't handle being confronted anymore. So they went out without me, afraid that I would judge them.

Once again, my guilt-motivated sobriety didn't last long. By the end of that visit, I was drinking with them, starting with nonalcoholic beer, then wine coolers, followed by vodka and everything else I could get my hands on.

Blair was dead. Life had stopped. Everything was gone. I couldn't deal with that. With Blair's passing, I finally knew that things would never be like they used to be. Even our beloved Tega Cay house next door to them had burned down some five years prior. Everything from the Heritage days was officially gone. Along with my hope, another part of me died that day.

When I got back from the funeral, I confessed to Mike that I'd consumed alcohol when I was out of town.

"I knew it," he said.

I'm sure he was tipped off by the guilt I wore on my face, but that kind of thing freaked me out. I thought that God had put a wire to Mike's head: Jay's sinning, Jay's looking at a girl's butt, Jay's drinking, Jay's touching himself.

"You're not doing what you need to," Mike told me. "What's wrong with you?"

Revolution had begun to heal me and give me direction. As I began to make peace with what had happened to my family, it was easier to carry the message my family had preached. I realized that I too had been called by God to show people the love of Christ and offer them an alternative to a church that didn't accept them.

That had changed my life. But I still hadn't recovered from the pain of my dad's being in prison or that things hadn't worked once he got out. I couldn't get over feeling that the Lord hated me. Being unable to meet Mike's expectations only made matters worse. So I decided to open the gates and be vulnerable with him, let him see my weakness, hurts, and pains.

"Mike, I'm still going through a really hard time," I said. "I haven't completely dealt with the PTL stuff, I haven't completely dealt with my dad getting out of prison. I even lived with my dad, and it didn't work out. The more and more I try to put on this show for everybody, the harder it gets to hide this stuff. It's coming back, and I can't stop it. I've got to deal with it."

I started to cry.

"Get over it, Jay. Everyone's got problems. I'm going through a hard time too!" he shot back harshly. "I've got this thing with Lloyd." (Lloyd was the head guy from Master's Commission, who at the time was trying to limit that organization's connection with Revolution.)

"Yeah, Mike, but this is different. This is my life. I've done nothing but live this since I was eleven years old. I just want to deal with it."

"How dare you compare problems! How dare you compare your pain to mine! Who are you to say how big a problem is?"

All I could think of was hundreds of lacerating newspaper articles and mocking *Saturday Night Live* skits. I flashed on sitting down with my dad to tell him that Mom was divorcing him. Not to downplay Mike's conflict, but I was dealing with my whole life here—major things that were causing me to break down and not be able to function—and I was in utter chaos. I needed someone to say, "All right, cry, man. I understand it hurts." Or, "I don't understand, but hurt, get mad, cry, yell, scream." Mike wasn't willing to do that.

I became so unhappy at Revolution, I couldn't even get through prayer with them anymore. By way of response, they would tell me to pray more. So I would go up to the church and pray for an hour straight.

"God deliver me," I'd pray. "God, show me what You want me to do. Show me the answer. Lead me to where You need me to go. Take me out of this valley."

Little did I know that there was more of a valley to come.

I started to think about leaving. Dad was to be the focus of a retreat in Hendersonville, North Carolina, intended to help restore him to the ministry. I had to do something, and I'd promised to attend. Besides, I knew Donnie Earl would be there, and I hadn't seen him in way too long.

The night before I left, Kelli and I sat outside on the front porch. Lit only by the moonlight, everything had that blue-haze feeling and look. The air was warm, with a nice night breeze, and the stars were bright. The peace of our surroundings, however, belied how burned out I felt.

"I just can't stand this anymore," I confessed. "I feel as if I don't even have a place here anymore. I just live in guilt every day, and I'm tired of it. Kelli, I don't think I'm going to stay."

Basically, I was just thinking out loud. I certainly didn't intend to leave right away. But God had other plans. The next day, I got on an airplane, fully expecting to return in a week. I wouldn't get back there for six months, and then it would be just for a visit.

A dozen pastors had initially been expected at Dad's retreat. Seventy showed up.

I addressed the full assembly on that first night. Not even trying to control my tears, I talked about my anger toward the church and how it treated the very people it was supposed to minister to.

"This isn't Jesus," I exclaimed. "This isn't what the Bible teaches."

I wanted them to remember Jesus' teachings, that we should abandon the unimportant trappings of religion in order to meet real people where they really are. Mostly, however, I talked about how the condemnation of a minister impacted not only him, but his family, and especially his kids, and about the lack of restoration for people in the church, which my family had felt so harshly. Though some tried to dismiss me as just another angry young man, my words touched others. At least that's what they told me.

Despite the confidence I displayed publicly, I remained a confused mess.

"I just feel if I smoke a cigarette, drink a beer, or have a lustful thought, God's going to hate me," I told Donnie Earl a couple of nights later.

"Jay, that's a bunch of nonsense," he retorted heatedly. "Who have you been hanging around with?"

I had gotten to the point where I was even scared to hear cuss words. But my protests didn't stop Donnie Earl.

"You're trying to make yourself good enough to please God," he said.

"Of course I am," I thought. "Isn't that what you're supposed to do?"

I was miserable, of course, and hadn't experienced any of the freedom in Christ that everyone talked about. But I didn't consider that.

"You're trying to earn your salvation, and you can't do that," Donnie Earl continued. "If you want a cigarette, smoke a cigarette." Then he drove me down to the gas station and bought me a pack. We continued to talk while I smoked one cigarette after another. Little did I know that the message of grace he was sharing with me would change the rest of my life.

"You know, if you ever wanted to come back and live with us, we'd love to have you," Donnie Earl offered.

That was just what I'd been thinking about. Though Dad was insisting that I should continue doing ministry in Phoenix, I knew I couldn't go back.

At the end of the retreat, as Donnie Earl and I sat in the back, splashing fiery citronella candle wax at each other and basically acting stupid, one of the more important pastors

there announced that it was time for the two of us to be rec-
ognized as ministers and ordained.

"Today, God has won the battle," the pastor said. "Jay, God
and Satan have been battling for your soul for a very long
time, but today God has won that battle."

How ironic! Not only had I just decided to quit the ministry, I was about to suffer my biggest crisis of faith ever.

Somewhere deep inside I knew that God was speaking
through that man and that God had a plan. But I would need
to go through more struggles and preparation time before I
would be ready, for my ministry would come through my
own brokenness.

12

Restoration

I moved back to the Paulks' house in Atlanta, having convinced some folks to pack my stuff, sell my car, and send me the money, which amounted to a whopping five hundred dollars. My parents had taught me that God was love, but despite the generosity and kindness of a few, I certainly hadn't seen much of that in the church at large. To the contrary. My family had been destroyed. PTL had been destroyed. And now my attempts to answer the Lord's calling had been destroyed by my repeated inability to live by His laws. Convinced that I'd screwed up my last chance and that God couldn't possibly ever love me now, I did my best to leave Him behind.

I started drinking heavily again. I didn't have many friends in Atlanta, but I'd go out to the clubs and get wasted with the few I did know, or go over to people's houses sometimes and raid their liquor cabinets. At one point, while visiting Bo in Orlando, I literally stayed drunk for three days straight. I might have gotten three or four hours of sleep during that entire time. Even all that alcohol did nothing to dull the heavy pain. It was as if my chest were ready to explode.

Soon I was blacking out again.

Instead of reprimanding, Donnie Earl made sure he was there for me. He would even accompany me to the bars, where I'd get drunk and start witnessing to everyone I could get my hands on.

"Get over here, darn it. I want to tell you about Jesus," I'd insist, trying hard not to slur. "Whatever you're doing, Jesus loves you."

Of course, I still didn't believe that for myself. Still, Donnie Earl hung in there.

The day I found out that my mom had colon cancer, I announced that instead of helping out with the youth group as I was supposed to, I was going over to a friend's house to get drunk.

"Okay, just wait for me to get there afterward so I can drive you home," Donnie Earl said.

He didn't tell me to get my act together or that I needed to be at church. Instead of trying to change me, he trusted God in my life. That's really how I was set free.

Over the months that followed, Donnie Earl shared his

own battles and struggles with me, so I would know that my doubts and slips were normal. And he showed me the love of Christ.

I was so certain that God couldn't—and wouldn't—ever love me because of the things I was doing that Donnie Earl's message about salvation and grace seemed little more than a compromise that excused sin. Eventually, however, I was so torn apart that I squelched my doubts and went along with his justification. If it gave me a little peace, it would do just fine.

"Jesus loves you no matter what," Donnie Earl continued to remind me. "You can't earn your salvation. That's a free gift, because Jesus died on the cross for your sins. Renouncing that free gift of salvation—grace—basically amounts to saying that He didn't need to die on the cross and that His death was in vain."

His words made me long to be with God and to really seek the truth.

"You've got to prove this to me," I told him. "If this is the truth, prove it."

So he did.

"Colossians 1:20 talks about how we're saved by what Christ did for us on the cross, and we are made holy and blameless in His sight," he told me. "Read the book of Romans. Read the book of Corinthians, Ephesians, Galatians."

I started with Ephesians. That's when I finally realized how much Jesus loves us. This whole time I'd had it wrong. I read scriptures like Ephesians 2:8–9:

We're saved by grace, not by works, so no man may boast.

Then I went on to Romans 3:22–25:

We are made right in God's sight when we trust in Jesus Christ to take away our sins. And we all can be saved in this same way, no matter who we are or what we have done. *For all have sinned, all have fallen short of God's glorious standard. Yet now God in His gracious kindness declares us not guilty. He has done this through Christ Jesus, who has freed us by taking away our sins. For God sent Jesus to take the punishment for our sins, and to satisfy God's anger against us. We are made right with God when we believe that Jesus shed His blood, sacrificing His life for us.*

It wasn't about whether I was drinking or not drinking, I discovered to my amazement. It was about accepting the free gift of salvation and falling in love with Jesus.

Grace is a gift that bounces off most people, because when you become obsessed with the outer process—with works—you simply tend to reflect the culture around you instead of transforming it. But everything I'd gone through, from my dad's going to prison to my own loss of faith, had finally prepared me for the message that God loves you no matter what. That didn't mean that there wouldn't be consequences for your actions during your lifetime and that you wouldn't be held accountable by your fellow human beings. But in God's eyes, you didn't have to be perfect. Paul, I discovered, talks at length about how he struggled with sin every single day and lost some of those battles. (Romans 7:14.) Galatians 5:17 says we are never free from the conflict of our nature to sin.

I started to realize that God loved me for who I was, not for what I could do for Him. I realized that if Jesus loved me so much, he must have so much more in store for me.

I couldn't wait to share what I was learning with Dad, who was still living alone in the mountain cabin.

"Dad, I can't believe this. God really does love us," I'd tell him during phone conversations that usually took place in the middle of the night after I'd just read some new passages. Sitting on Donnie Earl's big king-size bed in the red and green manly-man plaid room that used to be his, I'd read him those scripture passages I'd just discovered.

"Son, sometimes I have such a hard time accepting God's love because of the way I was raised in the church," he'd say.

When my dad was a little boy, they had had this picture of a big eye up on his Sunday school's wall near the ceiling with the words "Be careful little eye what you see, be careful little feet where you go." A kid's song about that "eye . . .

looking down on you, you, you" reinforced the notion that God was up there waiting to knock him out with a big stick.

At the end of his show, Dad would always tell viewers, "God loves you. He really does." And he really believed that. But he still had a difficult time believing that God loved *him*.

"God uses no perfect people," I told Dad. "Paul had Christians arrested and killed, Peter would deny Jesus three times and was so hot-headed that he couldn't control his temper and cut a guard's ear off. One of Jesus' best friends was Mary Magdalene, a prostitute. He had a reputation for befriending sinners. God loves you. Period."

Dad listened. He heard. And he too was set free.

Despite the redeeming message about grace that I'd received from Donnie Earl and shared with my dad, I couldn't shake the harsh depression that engulfed me. I'd tumbled into a huge abyss upon leaving Revolution. For starters, I was no longer doing any ministry to speak of. And I'd really started drinking heavily again. That just made things worse. I'd come home so drunk that I wouldn't be able to get the key in the door. Unwilling to wake Donnie Earl or his family, I'd be forced to wait outside until I was sober enough to get in the house.

When I finally made it to my room, I would just lie on the bed and cry. Anytime I was alone, a sense of hopelessness would descend over me, whether I was in the shower or outside smoking a cigarette. I felt like a loser. Regardless of what Donnie Earl told me again and again, I couldn't completely escape all those years of religious tradition and the belief that I was a disappointment to God.

I thought about killing myself. Only my fear of hell prevented me.

After six months, I realized that I had to get some help. So I started to see Jackie, the therapist, again.

"Jay, I think you're an alcoholic," he said bluntly.

The last time I'd been in Atlanta, I had accompanied a close friend to a twelve-step meeting. Once there, I promptly refused to acknowledge that I had an alcohol problem. Even though every single person there disagreed with me, I didn't think anything of it. Now here it was again.

Once again, I denied the charge totally, over sessions that lasted two to three hours.

"No way, man. I'm not an alcoholic. You're crazy," I'd tell him. "Jackie, I'm *not* an alcoholic. I don't drink every day. I drink on the weekends or every other day. There's no way."

"Let me just take you to one meeting," Jackie said. "It'll be a lunch meeting at Steak and Ale. There'll be no pressure."

"Okay," I agreed, to appease him. "I'm not an alcoholic, but I'd be more than happy to go to a meeting with you."

As we took our seats in the room, with its exposed wooden beams and picture windows, a slick, twenty-something yuppie turned to me.

"Run," he advised. "Run out of these rooms as fast as you can, because drinking for the rest of your life will be ruined."

Sometimes I wish to God I'd listened to him and that I could still allow myself to drink. Because thirty to forty minutes into the meeting, I knew Jackie and the others from that first meeting were right.

"Oh God, I'm an alcoholic," I realized. "I had no idea."

I got my white chip that day, which meant that I was to surrender and begin my first day sober. For the next month, the only way I managed to stay sober was to tell myself that I would have a drink tomorrow, a message I repeated the next day and then the day after that. I also relied heavily on the support I received from program members.

"The church could sure learn a lot from this model," I thought to myself, fully aware of how ironic that was.

But for me, faith and sobriety were integrally related. Grace made me want to stop drinking. And the clear, unclouded mind that resulted contributed immeasurably to my own relationship with God. Each one made the other possible.

I'd been clean for thirty days when Donnie Earl asked me to preach to his church's youth group of about four hundred kids. When he called me up to the stage, I looked out at that crowd and froze. Terrified, I saw hundreds of impatient kids watching me.

I opened up my Bible, tried to recollect what I'd written out in all the long notes I'd made for myself, and started to talk. It didn't help. I got more and more nervous and less and less able to collect my thoughts. Then a group of kids to my left started talking. Here I was preaching about grace, and these kids were talking!

"Shut the hell up, you guys!" I finally yelled. "You don't know how hard it is to speak up here."

When I was finally done, Donnie Earl got up and untangled my convoluted sermon. It took him about twenty minutes to straighten it all out.

Afterwards, one mom came up to me.

"I needed to hear that so bad, and so did my son who's here with me," she said.

I didn't know what she heard or what she meant. I thanked her and silently vowed never to preach again.

13

The Sober Truth

Since I wasn't going to school or doing ministry, I decided I should get a job. Even though I declared my intention of dying my hair blue, the Gap hired me right away.

When I wasn't working, I focused on getting sober. I started going to ten o'clock meetings at a twelve-step clubhouse, where I met this skater who was into hip-hop. Afterwards, we'd go play pool and talk about all the girls at the meetings we were too afraid to talk to.

The fact was that as soon as I stopped drinking, I could no longer talk to girls. For the most part, I couldn't really talk to anyone I didn't already know.

Though I spent a lot of time by myself—skateboarding, driving the streets, and smoking cigarettes—Donnie Earl and I continued our late-night discussions about grace and Jesus.

"Aren't these people compromising?" I kept asking myself. "Isn't grace just a free license to sin?"

Still, I felt closer to Christ than I ever had before, blown away by that unconditional love and acceptance. By late summer 1996, I started to feel that I should share these newly discovered gifts.

Tommy Reid, a pastor out of Buffalo, New York, whom I truly respected, had offered me a position as his assistant youth pastor. My dad wanted me to do it so badly he could barely stand it. They had a Bible college up there that I thought I should be part of once I got my GED. So I had pretty much decided to move to New York, especially since the Paulks were relocating and I would no longer be able to stay at their place.

I felt that God was showing me the perfect, logical choice. Then I got a call from a friend of my dad's, an Irish preacher named Bob Gass.

"You're going to go up to New York, and those guys aren't going to be able to handle you," he said with his thick Irish accent. "You still like to go to clubs and hang out, you're into punk rock, you dye your hair blue, and you've got earrings and tattoos. You're too crazy for them.

"I know somebody who you need to talk to in Atlanta: Philip Bray. You need to work with him."

The last time I'd lived with the Paulks, Donnie Earl had taken me to Philip Bray's inner-city ministry called Safehouse. That visit had impacted me in a major way. Though I'd moved away, the ministry had kept me on its mailing list. Those letters had helped prompt my decision to return to ministry.

There are just some things that are divine appointments in life, and this was one of them.

I went down to see Philip Bray, a stocky, gray-haired, Harley-driving pastor, the following week. After a tour of Safehouse, a red brick building located in downtown Atlanta, and Alpha House, a nearby facility where the homeless could eat, shower, and get their laundry done, we sat down outside on the curb.

"I've got to get back into ministry, or I'm going to die," I told Philip, lighting a cigarette. "I have to tell people about the grace and love of Jesus."

"I understand," he said.

"But I'm homeless here," I said. "I've got this offer to go to New York, so that's what I'll probably do."

"Jay, I will pay you two hundred and fifty dollars every two weeks and give you a place to live," Philip offered.

I thanked him for the offer, adding that I would probably wind up going to New York anyway.

When Pastor Bob drove me home that night, he argued vehemently against my going.

"They're just not ready for an assistant youth pastor who is going to clubs and smoking," he insisted.

When I told my dad that I couldn't decide what to do, he advised me to pray.

"God will open the door that's supposed to be open and close the door He doesn't want you to go through," he told me.

I agreed to trust God.

Time was running out at the Paulks. I only had two weeks left before their move, which was exactly when I was due in Buffalo. Then Pastor Reid from New York called to say that complications would delay my starting there for a month and a half. That wasn't going to work at all.

Remembering what my dad had said about God opening the right door and closing the wrong one, I called Philip.

"We're ready for you," he said.

So I packed all my stuff up and moved to a little house with barred windows that was surrounded by projects and located in one of the worst neighborhoods in Atlanta. I watched drug dealers make deals across the street. Dad came down to help me paint and fix up the house, including putting a dead bolt on my *bedroom* door.

I started working at Alpha House, washing homeless men's clothes, helping them get showers, working in the clothes closet, making and serving them food. We'd have to be there from seven in the morning till four in the afternoon. In addition, I tried, however ineffectually, to help Pastor Philip with his schedule of appearances. Still, I wasn't fulfilled.

Several weeks later, the pastor was invited to give his testimony at the If ministry coffeehouse located in Little Five Points, one of my favorite neighborhoods in Atlanta. He asked if I wanted to come along.

I met him there around six-thirty. We started talking to some guys and girls almost as soon as we sat down.

"Don't I know you from somewhere?" asked a beautiful blond with chameleon eyes who worked there. She'd seen me at the Gap. Even though she was clearly out of my range, that gave me an inroad. We started talking.

I began to spend as much time as I could at the ministry coffee shop, hanging out and helping with whatever needed to be done. The more I went, the more I started to really like Amanda—to the point where I got petrified around her. I was so scared, I probably smoked twice as many cigarettes as usual and talked a tenth as much. I figured as long as I was smoking, I didn't have to say anything (since the absence of alcohol continued to render me completely speechless around girls). I'd just act and look cool and try to pull a little James Dean on her.

We didn't exactly hit it off at first. When I told Amanda I liked her, she said our relationship could never work because I was too quiet. Little did she know!

Somehow I talked her into going out with me; soon we were dating. One of our favorite things to do was to buy Swisher Sweet or Black and Mild cigars and park our car over by the edge of this freeway, where we would look at the city and watch the cars go by while we smoked and talked.

Not long after we'd started seeing each other, my house got broken into. I called one of my friends, who happened to be Amanda's cousin. I didn't want to bother Amanda; our relationship was too new to burden her or mess things up between us. But since she and her cousin both lived in her mother's house, I couldn't help hoping that she might pick up the phone. She did. The next day, she came over to wait for the police with me. The cops never showed up to take the stolen property report, but Amanda and I kissed for the first time that day.

Once again, though I had continued working with Pastor Philip and had even started speaking a little on my own, I felt as if my life was never really going to happen. Feeling completely stressed over the lack of direction, I tried to forget my troubles by sleeping the days away. I rarely went to work. When I was there, I felt downright useless.

I went to Philip.

"I don't know what to do with myself," I confessed.

Instead of firing me, Philip made an appointment for me with David C. Cooper, the new pastor at Mount Paran Church of God, which had helped support Safehouse. I didn't want to see the pastor alone, so Philip went with me. Just as Jesus saw the potential in Peter and said, "You will be my rock," I think Philip saw what God was going to raise up in me and help me become.

He may have believed in me, but I still didn't believe in myself.

Still, I told the Mount Paran pastor all about Revolution. "But now I feel lazy," I told him. "There's nothing I can do."

"You're not lazy. There's nothing wrong with you," he told me. "You just lack purpose."

That hit me. Over the years, so many people had told me that I was lazy and just playing around that I believed them. But maybe he was right. Maybe all I was missing was my purpose!

"Let's just pray that God's going to help you find your purpose," Pastor Cooper said.

On our way home, I grabbed a flyer for Edgefest, a music festival that Mount Paran Church of God was putting on. It was one of the cheesiest flyers I'd ever seen: totally Christian-y and pink. The next day I took it apart and redesigned it to make it look insane, using images and lettering I clipped out from magazines. I worked on it for hours.

"What are you doing?" Philip asked when he walked in. I explained.

"Maybe you're starting to find your purpose," he said with a smile.

PART FOUR

Carrying

The

Message

14

Sharing the Truth

The last few months had revealed how much I still needed to find out about myself. Newly sober and facing life's realities—and emotions—for the first time, I was desperate to do something for God. I knew that He had given me a powerful calling for my life, but I had a hard time putting my finger on what that calling was.

The one thing about which I was still certain was that something was missing from what the church was offering people like me. Watered-down or turn-or-burn versions of what had been preached in decades past were being tendered, but most preachers weren't really reaching kids with a message of hope or grace. The fact was that few had done the hard work of changing the message to touch today's youth, especially today's disenfranchised youth.

I still wanted to step in and help fill that gap. I just didn't know how.

Then I got a call from Bobby Murray, the Mount Paran youth pastor, asking me to meet with him. We met for lunch at the Vortex, a popular bar and grill with a fifteen-foot skull as its entrance.

"We're doing this festival called Edgefest," he said once we'd ordered.

Since I'd helped redesign their flier, I already knew that. His next words, however, surprised and disconcerted me. As it turned out, the people who were running the festival didn't want an edgy band like those on the Tooth and Nail label. They simply felt they weren't "Christian" enough. Rumors about different bands' lifestyles fed their determination to exclude them.

I knew all too well how rumors and gossip, however unfounded, could destroy people. I wasn't about to let that go.

"That's ridiculous," I said. "If you want to reach non-Christians or anyone from my scene, you're gonna have to have these bands."

"You've got to come to the next board meeting," Bobby exclaimed. "This is awesome."

From that moment on, Bobby and I became tight. He would later be my best man at my wedding.

A few days later, I met with the Edgefest board to talk about booking these bands, being relevant to my culture, and the importance of not judging them. These bands, composed of young Christians, were continuously getting dumped on over ridiculous rumors.

"We've got to encourage these people instead of turning our backs on them," I insisted. "They're reaching a part of my generation that no one else is."

I didn't know how my sentiments would be received. But after much discussion, they agreed to allow me to book a few bands for their second stage.

To encourage these bands even more, I decided to give each band member a leather New Living Bible. I had discovered great strength in the Bible and especially in that translation. I wanted to share that.

After much begging and pleading, Tyndale House publishers donated two hundred of their nicest Bibles. I was ecstatic. Over the next few months, I'd give those Bibles, along with a note saying how much I appreciated their ministry, to bands coming through town. Even if they weren't mentioning the gospel, even if they didn't know it, these musicians were still doing ministry since they were encouraging the kids who listened to them. Most of the band members were really pleased by the gift.

"At least I'm finally doing something to help people," I thought.

It was a start.

A few days later, just a week after meeting with Pastor Cooper from the Mount Paran Church of God, Amanda and I were walking around Little Five Points, that small neighborhood in Atlanta where punk kids congregate. Though Amanda had decided that she wanted to go off to college, we were getting pretty serious. As we talked about the future, the conversation veered right back to the one question that had been popping up more and more: What was our purpose in life?

Between counseling sessions and new opportunities— like the Mount Paran Church of God asking me to act as a consultant for their festival once they saw the flier I'd redesigned—I was honing in on some general answers. The specifics, however, remained a disconcerting blur.

All of a sudden, as we strolled past this big empty storefront, it came to me.

"You could really do something in this place, like turn it into a club," I mused. "That's it! That's my purpose. I need to start something. I need to start a Revolution here."

Revolution was the perfect concept for what I envisioned. I'd always loved Mike Wall's explanation of how he came up with the name "Revolution." In the 1970s, when the hippie movement was at its height, a lot of barefoot kids came to Jesus in response to Calvary Chapel's outreach.

"What about the carpet?" worried the church's elders. "These kids are going to ruin the carpet with their dirty feet."

"This is a house of God," the pastor responded. "You're worried about the carpet? We'll take the carpet out then."

The Jesus movement was pretty radical. But like any movement, it moved and then it stopped. A revolution is ongoing, providing continuous, constant motion that never ceases. And, man, do we need one.

Just recently, quoting the Old Testament from Leviticus 19:28, a TV pastor labeled pierced and tattooed kids as people of the devil. But he failed to mention that this old covenant law, which predates Christ's arrival and the new covenant He established, also dictates that people not cut their sideburns, trim their beards, or wear clothes made of two kinds of fabric. If you're going to follow the law, you have to follow the whole law. You can't just pick and choose the portions you like. Since this preacher is very well groomed, with no beard and with itty-bitty sideburns, that's exactly what he was doing.

That kind of misinterpretation of the scriptures is turning a whole generation away from God. That's why we as the church are losing the battle. While people are hurting, dying—and even killing—some ministers point fingers at parents working all day, at video games, and Marilyn Manson, instead of looking at how religious closed-mindedness and tradition have contributed to the problem.

It only takes one act of defiance to start a revolution, and I suddenly knew what I wanted mine to be. Instead of trying to mold kids into a supposedly Christian image, I would accept them the way they were. Period. There would be no question of time limits or readiness. I would love them as completely as God loves us and would never give up on them. And that would absolutely fly in the face of most of what I've personally experienced as the church's practices today.

I called Mike Wall. Over the past few months, we had started to heal the breach between us. The bond of our ministry had proven stronger than the misunderstandings of the past. He greeted my news with pure excitement. We had always dreamed of taking Revolution across the country, even around the world. He couldn't have been more supportive.

In order to start a Revolution in Atlanta, I had to find like-minded allies who would help lay the same kind of foundation we'd established in Phoenix. In addition, while coming up with different ideas for the ministry, I started trying to recruit kids with fliers and in person. For the latter, I headed straight back to the clubs—not to drink this time, but to explain what Revolution was and that it would be coming soon. I also started developing my mailing list and sending out a monthly letter about Revolution, how it was progressing and what we were thinking about doing.

I put together a meeting of all the pastors I really respected—Donnie Earl, my dad, Tommy Reid, Bishop Paulk, Philip Bray, and Pastor Jack Wolf—to introduce my vision to them. Each one received a box I'd put together containing a booklet about Atlanta Revolution's purpose and goals, photos from

Phoenix Revolution along with different flyers showing the various ways we'd reached kids, and a Revolution T-shirt I'd designed. Mike Wall even flew down for a few days.

That weekend, Dad told me about a place out in Los Angeles ministering to the inner city that he was considering becoming a part of.

"Why don't you think about starting a Revolution out there?" he asked.

Neither Mike Wall, who had come down to speak at Edgefest, nor I were really hip on that idea.

"Just don't take Revolution out there," Mike told me.

"Yeah, I know," I replied. "If a Revolution ever starts in California, Kelli needs to do it, because it's always been in her heart to start a Revolution out there. So don't worry about it. We'll never take a Revolution out to Los Angeles."

We should have knocked on a big old piece of wood, because I ended up in L.A. before you knew it.

Four weeks after Edgefest, Amanda left for college in Mississippi, where her sister was already a student. I had a real hard time with her leaving, because I'd really fallen in love with her by then. But she wanted a few weeks to get herself settled, and my dad wanted me to visit him in Los Angeles, so I flew to California for a week. Once there, I ran into two women, Denise and Monique, who used to run Scrape Productions, the agency that had booked all the bands for Revolution.

"Man, we would love to have a Revolution out here," they said.

I didn't think much about it, since I was just visiting.

It's weird how God does things. After my return, my dad kept talking to me about moving out. With Amanda gone, life wasn't the same in Atlanta. Then everyone in the house I was renting decided to move. I no longer had a way to stay in Atlanta and had to relocate as well.

When I told Philip I was moving to Los Angeles, he gave me a national pager.

"I want to let you know I'll be here for you if you ever need me," he said. "Safehouse wants to support you and keep you on staff. You can always be His hands extended."

Christ's Hands Extended was their logo. So even though I was leaving his ministry, I would represent Safehouse out in Los Angeles.

Before leaving, I went to Mississippi and spent time with Amanda. I couldn't help feeling scared about what would happen to our relationship with us being so far apart.

"We'll stay close," I swore, trying not to sound as hopeless as I felt.

Then I drove my car across country, listening as I drove to some New Living Bible tapes I'd purchased. I started at Matthew. By the time I pulled into Los Angeles, I was listening to the book of Revelation.

The idea was to start a Revolution in Los Angeles with Kelli, who had moved out as well. But though we made a lot of relationships with different kids and wound up holding one of our biggest concerts ever, Revolution never really took off in Los Angeles. I think it had a lot to do with the fact that we were too radical for the church we were working under.

Dad and I took up residence in an old nunnery located on church grounds, while Kelli lived across the street. With Dad's and my rooms connected by the bathroom, we were finally living together again. Every morning Dad would come in to my room and eat cereal, since that's where he had set up a refrigerator and breakfast table. Even though I was still trying to sleep, he would turn on the light, plunk his silverware down on the table, and chomp his cereal so loudly it drove me crazy.

It didn't make any difference. I was so excited that my dad was out of prison and that we were together again. To me, that was fantastic—tops. Despite the sparse living arrangements, we were managing to get along on a personal level.

Working with the church, however, proved incredibly frustrating. Dad was doing all he could to help make the building look less like a cold institution. But there were so many chiefs and so few Indians that you had to put in a request for something as basic as a ladder or a can of paint and then wait two days.

People fought him tooth and nail on everything. That was hard for me to watch. I felt they didn't respect my father for all he had done in his life for the Christian community. Even in a place of supposed restoration, most could not see past my dad's failures. They'd bring him on TV every once in a while when they needed publicity, but otherwise they kept him at a distance.

On my side, here I was a grace pastor, totally believing in the unconditional love of Christ. By night, I would study the book of Romans in depth, but during the day I found myself embroiled in a lot of unnecessary pettiness.

I remember reaching out to two traveler kids who had worked with Revolution in Phoenix and needed a place to stay. The Los Angeles church's policy, however, was that if you were going to stay there, you needed to work thirty hours a week.

"These kids don't have much of a work ethic right now," I argued. "They're hippies who have been on the road. You can't give them a work ethic overnight—it takes time to help people."

"The 1970s are over. Those kids need to get cleaned up and take a shower. We were going to have them work in the kitchen, but they're too dirty. Just tell them to leave and go home."

So instead of doing ministry, I had to kick these kids out!

The pettiness continued. The head of security even had a forklift pick up Kelli's car and move it from the ministry parking area to a dumpster while we were away at Tom Fest, a music festival in Oregon. They were about to have it towed when we got back.

"How was I supposed to know?" the head of security argued.

"There's a Revolution sticker on the car," I answered angrily.

"How am I supposed to know that?"

"Look at the car. Look for signs that maybe it belongs to someone you know," I replied. "My dad used to run a huge ministry—thousands of people. One thing he always focused on was being kind to people and putting them first. It is ridiculous how you treat people here. You should learn from my dad."

"Your dad built that ministry, and we all saw what happened to him," the head of security countered.

Throwing that in my face really hurt my feelings and made it even harder to stay there.

"Oh, it just takes time," the pastor said when I told him about what had happened. "We're working out bugs."

I don't have any clue about what it is to run a ministry that size, though I'm starting to understand the challenge of working with people more and more as my own ministry grows. But as a church, we've got to start putting people first no matter what. We can't kick people out for saying a few cuss words or smoking a joint or getting angry. We've got to trust

God in their lives. Anything less is conditional love, when we really serve a God who loves us unconditionally. In 1 Corinthians 13:7, it talks about how love never gives up, never loses faith, is always hopeful, and endures through every circumstance. Like others in the church at large, these church leaders were not demonstrating endurance through trying circumstances.

They had a hard time accepting my dad. Imagine if Paul the Apostle, who had persecuted Christians, had come there to set up a ministry—they would have labeled him unworthy and a Christian killer and thrown him out. Or David, who had a man killed because he wanted the man's wife. Yet Jesus didn't see the struggles of those in front of Him; He saw their potential. He loved them despite sins and faults.

Amid troubles with the church in Los Angeles and yet another disappointment with Revolution, I did manage to complete the paperwork that would lead to my ordination by the American Evangelistic Association some eight months later. I had also continued giving out Bibles to touring bands. (I'll never forget giving one to Mike Ness, Social Distortion's lead singer, at the Roxy on L.A.'s Sunset Strip.)

And on the personal front, in August, Amanda, who had moved to Los Angeles in May 1998, told me that she would marry me. She had been watching P.O.D. (a Christian rock band) during a three-day music festival called Tom Fest, which we'd driven out to see, when the Lord confirmed that we would be wed. My heart swelled.

Earlier that year, the Cornerstone music festival in Bushnell, Illinois, also proved life-changing. I'd been walking outside the concert area on a dirt road, feeling hot and gross from sweating all day, when I slipped in a mud puddle. Half covered in muck and ticked off, I walked into a tent where the band Pedro the Lion was playing and made my way to the front. I didn't know what to expect. Suddenly, the band started to play a song called "The Secret of the Easy Yolk":

> I could hear church bells ringing,
> They pealed aloud your praise.
> The members' faces were smiling,
> With their hands outstretched to shake.
> It's true they did not move me,
> My heart was hard and tired.
> Their perfect fire annoyed me,
> I could not find you anywhere.
>
> Could someone please tell me the story
> Of sinners ransomed from the fall?
> I still have never seen you,
> And some days I don't love you at all.
>
> The devoted were wearing bracelets
> To remind them why they came,

Concrete motivation when abstract could not do the
same.
But if all that's left is duty,
I'm falling on my sword.
At least then, I would not serve an unseen, distant Lord.

Could someone please tell me the story
Of sinners ransomed from the fall?
I still have never seen you.
Some days I don't love you at all.

If this is only a test, I hope that I'm passing,
Because I'm losing steam.
I still want to trust you.
Peace be still,
Peace be still,
Peace be still,
Peace be still.

That song broke my heart. It reminded me of my life and
my own experience with the church. The lyrics were so bru-
tally honest, confirming to me that others felt as I did. My life
seemed to flash before my eyes. The lead singer, David Bazan,
had put into words what I had felt for so long.

It also reminded me of "What Would Jesus Do?" bracelets,
the "I Am Going to Stay a Virgin" contracts, and the promise

rings that people get by making a commitment not to have sex until they're married. There's nothing wrong with living a good life. To the contrary. But all these things focus on duty and works so much that the message of Christ gets lost. Salvation is not about works. It never has been.

People think of the Antichrist as some six-horned beast that's going to come and take over the world. But having thirty thousand kids in a stadium signing contracts saying that they will never sin again embodies the spirit of the Antichrist, a spirit that is alive and well right now in the American church. In their efforts to earn God's favor, the kids are saying that they can do it on their own, thereby rendering Christ's death useless. Galatians 2:21 says:

> I am not one of those who treats the grace of God as meaningless, for if we could be saved by keeping the law then there was no need for Christ to die.

Salvation is free. All we have to do is accept Jesus. You see it is only Christ working in us that causes us to lose our tendency to sin. But we've become so caught up in signing contracts and doing what we've decided is right, we're not showing—or seeing—Jesus anymore. We're simply managing our sins, which in turn encourages the church's judgmental nature.

15

Grace for the Tortured

At the time I needed God and the church most, I was driven away from both. Now that I started to read God's word, I realized that so much of the church has made up rules that are nowhere to be found in the Bible or taken the scriptures out of context and turned them into traditions. Meanwhile, the Christian Right's legalistic militancy has created an ideal that's impossible to live up to. In both cases, a lack of tolerance dictates behavior that seems downright un-Christlike.

The last straw for me happened at a church in Los Angeles that had been heralded for its openness. Amanda, Kelli, Kelli's sister Kacee, and I had been feeling so burned out from all the bickering in Los Angeles that we decided to go for some solace to the very church where the Jesus movement had been born. Though thirty years had passed since then and the movement has largely vanished, we figured that this was surely a church where we'd fit in and be accepted, where we could just relax and hear about Jesus.

When we arrived at the church, an overzealous usher grabbed Kelli's arm and pulled her back outside because of the water bottle she was carrying. We were a little freaked out, but left the water bottle with him and went in anyway.

The pastor's sermon included a comment about molestation that deeply offended Kelli's sister, who had lived a painful life. She stormed out of the church, and Kelli, who was seated a couple of people down, hadn't noticed her leave. Wanting to let Kelli know what was going on, I motioned for her to come outside with me.

"Okay, we'll see you later," one of the ushers said as I followed her out the door.

"No, I'll be right back," I answered. "I just have to tell my staff member something."

"I'm sorry, sir," he said. "You can't come back in here."

"I'm a pastor. I've got a couple of people with me," I said. "We just came here tonight to enjoy the service, but I've got to impart some information to my staffer."

"You can come back in, but you won't be able to go back in the service," he insisted.

"My girlfriend's in there," I said.

"Sir, can't your girlfriend take care of herself?" he countered.

I'd had enough. I ran outside to update Kelli about her sister and this newest development. When I got out there, one of the ushers was yelling at Kacee for smoking.

"Wait a second," I thought to myself. "I thought this was supposed to be the big come-as-you-are '70s church." Maybe the 1980s, with all its underpinnings of prosperity thinking, along with the influence of the right-wing conservatives and the dogma all that created, had tarnished this as well.

I think all churches should have a place where they allow smoking, or at least allow smoking outside. We've got to say "Come as you are," not "Come cleaned up and perfect and tidy." If Jesus is willing to meet people where they're at, we should be too. People should be more important than rules.

I had to bully my way back into the service to get Amanda. I don't know if they were treating us differently because we looked different and had piercings and tattoos, but I had sure been expecting a better reception from a church known for reaching out to radical people. My heart broke as I walked out for the last time. If we couldn't be accepted here, then where?

Hurt and profoundly disillusioned, I could have given up at that point. But Jesus found me. So instead of turning away from religion, Kelli and I strengthened our resolve to start Revolution. There simply needed to be a place where all people could come and be accepted the way they were, a place they could walk in and walk out of, where they could stand up and say, "I totally disagree with you."

Shortly thereafter, we returned to Atlanta to visit. While there, we met with Philip Bray, who had continued to support me the whole time I'd been away.

"Philip, I would love to come back here, but I'd have to be able to answer only to you," I said, trying to feel out the possibilities. "Kelli and I would have to be paid staff. We'd need our own office, and we'd need our own night to do a service."

I really wasn't expecting anything. Amazingly, he agreed to all my requests.

Life was about to change for me once again—and for my dad as well.

I had met Lori Graham, a friend of Kelli's, in Phoenix while working at Revolution. "You remind me of my mother," I had told her then.

When Lori came down to visit Los Angeles, Amanda, Kelli, and I thought it would be a neat idea for her to meet my dad. She just seemed like his type. Though my dad had dated a little, he hadn't hit it off with anyone. Still, we all thought that they would fall in love, and we were right. They married just a couple of months later.

Shortly thereafter, having spent almost a year in Los Angeles, Amanda and I loaded up the black Jeep I drove and headed home to Atlanta. By the time Kelli followed us a few months later, arriving toward the beginning of 1999, Amanda and I were engaged.

We were married by my dad on June 5 in a beautiful ceremony built around the themes of grace and the unconditional love of Christ. My sister got up and sang a rendition of "Amazing Grace" that will forever be etched in my soul. And for the first time in years, my mom, my dad, my sister, and I were all together.

On the ministry front, Kelli and I worked with Philip to get things ready for Revolution. We had a new message—that a personal relationship with Christ was right there within easy reach. Jesus is unconditional love. Period. If you accept the gift of salvation, He's willing to accept you. Period. It was a message that a generation of kids desperately needed to hear.

Atlanta's Revolution started with a bunch of us just hanging out in Little Five Points' stores and bars as well as tattoo and piercing parlors (where I've had most of my tattoo work and all of my piercings done). By the third month, when we introduced Tuesday night Bible study, the kids liked and trusted us. Though few of them attended our weekly sessions, more have come to our shows. And we continue to build friendships with them.

Though nobody showed up for our first three studies, thankfully kids from all over Atlanta eventually responded to what we were offering. They may have been pierced and tattooed, with shaved heads or purple hair, adorned with chains or black lipstick, dressed in black or army fatigues or barely covered at all, but they came to hear about God.

"You're a pastor?" a few outside individuals asked when they saw my tattoos, piercings, and dress. "You must be Satan's pastor."

That's exactly the attitude that has driven so many of my generation away. People don't hang out with those who are constantly on top of them, constantly rebuking them and asking them to change. Jesus knew that.

My goal was to build real friendships with a lot of people who, like me, felt they didn't fit in. I remember meeting a girl named Suzie who had been so hurt by the church that she professed to hate God. Somehow, we made a connection, for I realized that, like so many others who have been mistreated in the name of the Lord, she was just lashing out as I did.

Our efforts started to gain attention beyond our community. That winter, a freelance writer approached me about doing a magazine interview with *Good Housekeeping*. The article ended up being so short that she wanted to do a more in-depth piece. She mentioned a number of possibilities and asked what my number-one choice would be.

"*Rolling Stone,*" I answered promptly.

She assured me that was impossible. She was wrong.

When the *Rolling Stone* article showing me with all my tattoos hit the stands on September 16, 1999, bits of it got picked up by a number of other publications, including *Time* magazine. Soon my phone was ringing off the hook. As usual, some of the media focused on a few details taken out of context and then harassed me about them.

"It says here in the article that you can barely spell, that you have a hard time writing," one radio shock jock told me over the phone, having honed in on the fact that I have dyslexia. "You're white trash. Are you cut out for this job?"

"Oh no, not this again," I thought to myself.

But I knew the *Rolling Stone* article could speak for itself, and its readers were the very people I wanted to tell about the grace of Christ. So despite the fallout, I felt that I, a Bakker, had finally gotten a fair shake. And even though my family had yet to be fully restored, I felt like I was starting to be.

According to the dictionary, to "restore" means to bring back to a former or original condition. When something is restored in the Scriptures, however, it is always increased, multiplied, or improved so that its later state is significantly better than its original state. Even though Safehouse had really opened its arms to me, the world rather than the church was helping to restore me and my family—and God was using *Rolling Stone* magazine as His vehicle.

The week after the magazine hit the stands, seventy-five people showed up for our Bible study group. Though a lot of the kids hadn't read the article yet, they'd heard about it. And they came, some even stayed.

"This is a place where people can fit in, where they can feel comfortable," Justin Green, a twenty-nine-year-old with head-to-toe tattoos who works at a piercing parlor and initially showed up to Revolution drunk, told a reporter from the Gannett News Service. "Revolution isn't intimidating. It's a beginning."

From the start, Revolution has tried to build a foundation of grace and love, so people can have a personal relationship with Christ, so even if their church had told them they weren't good enough, they would realize that their salvation isn't based on the opinion of a pastor or anyone else around them. And even if they never went to church again, they'd know that Christ loves them very much.

That message reaches kids when nothing else does. The night a sixteen-year-old with fangs first showed up, I asked him to open his long black trench coat to make sure he wasn't carrying any weapons. It seemed as if nothing I said affected him in the least, but he kept coming back. One night after our Bible study, he asked to talk. We went downstairs to an empty room and conferred for an hour. Still nothing. A month later, we headed downstairs again.

"I want to be saved," he announced.

"Why do you want to come to Jesus?" I asked.

"Because I've never felt loved like this before," he

answered. "I now realize who Jesus is, and He is not the man my father made Him out to be."

Finally, he felt safe enough to accept God.

"Lord, don't ever let me get used to this," I prayed later.

I believe in people no matter how messed up they are. When I invited Justin to start attending Revolution's Tuesday night Bible study, he came, much to my surprise. Justin summed up the type of person I wanted to reach. Though he was drunk almost all the time, he had heard that Revolution was a place where he could get his life together. I talk to guys like that all the time. They rarely show up. Justin did, even if he was intoxicated. The few times he hadn't been drinking, he'd get the shakes. Still, we started to hang out. That's when I found out that an even more devastating addiction had hold of him. Even so, I saw God in Justin, and I didn't doubt that He has a great purpose for this young man.

Justin is starting to come around. I've helped him get a job, and he's living in a ministry house run by Revolution. Justin may never get free of his addictions. But even if he never gets his life straight, I will not give up on him. And I will never stop loving him. He has truly become one of my very best friends.

Ministering to people in our own way is what Revolution is all about. Instead of witnessing to people about Jesus, we get to know people where they're at, build a relationship, and lead by example. To me, being a silent witness and letting your actions speak for themselves is critical.

"Why does he eat with such scum?" the teachers of religious law asked when they saw Jesus sharing a meal with tax collectors, who were reviled for what was considered traitorous activity against their own people, and many other notorious sinners.

"Healthy people don't need a doctor, sick people do," Jesus countered. "I have come to call the sinner, not those who think they are already good enough." That's in Mark 2:17.

Of course, even though I've started coming into my own as a pastor—and a husband—it isn't always easy to remember the message of grace and love I preach where my own life is concerned. The last time I went to visit Heritage USA, I got kicked out for trespassing. Yes, the area had been posted as private property. Although the complex is overgrown and falling apart, I wanted to show Linden Gross, the writer helping me with this book, where I came from. And to be honest, despite the change in ownership, I can't help feeling that Heritage USA is my birthright. It's the place I grew up in and that in my own small way I helped create. My soul is still layered deep in its foundations, the little kid in me stuck in a holding pattern engendered by its loss. So we had to visit if Linden was to fully understand what I was all about.

I'd been there often in the past, always without incident. Not this time. Though we didn't know it, security vehicles began tracking us from the moment we drove past the gates and down the long drive that used to be so meticulously manicured. We pulled off behind the structure that used to be Kevin's House, built to house severely disabled children, in order to see the farm that Dad had built across the pond. I guess that's where we lost them. Then we drove up to the Grand Hotel, at daunting speeds of twelve to twenty miles an hour, and stopped to look around.

Three trucks finally managed to corner us over by what had once been the youth recreational area, complete with pool, skating rink, arts and crafts center, and pizza parlor. That was our first inkling they were trying to find us.

"My name is Jay Bakker," I said. "I just wanted to show my writer where I grew up."

"I'm sorry, Jamie Charles, but you're trespassing," said the beefy man who stopped us and who clearly knew exactly who I was. "We've been citing people for trespassing right and left."

I explained about the book once again.

"Can't we at least drive around? Can I at least show her the buildings I grew up in?" I asked, unable to hold back tears of frustration and hurt. "This was my family's, and it just got ripped away from us. I just want to show her my heritage."

Softening, the guard radioed in.

"Jamie Charles Bakker is on the premises and is asking permission to drive around," he said into his walkie-talkie.

"Negative. The area is posted," a woman's voice said after a minute's delay.

"If it were up to me, I'd let you go anywhere," the man said apologetically.

I sobbed so hard on the way back to my dad's house that I could scarcely drive. No one had ever been cruel enough to make me deal with the reality that I was no longer welcome in the place I still considered home.

After talking to my dad and sister, I drove over to Mom's.

"Aw, Honey, I'm so sorry that happened to you," she said. "But you've got to let it go. You've got to put a period on this."

Then looking on the bright side as only she can, she smiled.

"Well, at least they can't eat ya!"

A week later, I returned to Heritage USA, this time with my whole staff in tow. A friendly guard let us tour the entire complex, including our suite in the Grand Hotel, which remains eerily pristine amidst the other dilapidated buildings and the unkempt grounds. We ended up in the Upper Room, where partners could come to pray at any hour of the day or night. As my staff sat down on the pews that were still in place, I walked up to the table at the front and opened my Bible to read Romans 8:35–39 about how nothing, not trouble, calamity, or even the powers of hell, can separate us from Christ's love.

Standing in the middle of my dad's broken dreams, I looked out at the group in front of me—Amanda, my wonderful wife and best friend, who's pure happiness; Kelli, who helped start Revolution and functions as its heart, soul, and spine; Armando, a reformed gang member turned minister who serves as my dad's assistant; and the nine volunteers who comprise Revolution's staff and help make it run. Those include Kevin, who had been a straight-edge atheist just six months before I hired him.

"Look at what I have," I told them. "Everything I've gone through has been worth it just to be with you."

God's plan for my life was perfect. It was tortuous, but it paid off because we're now reaching people the church may never have been able to touch before. And I could never have connected with the hurting people in my ministry if I hadn't been alienated by society myself.

Kelli and I, with Pastor Philip Bray's help, are looking for a building for Revolution, a place where people would eventually be able to hang out twenty-four hours a day. Ideally, Revolution would feature regular shows, a coffee shop, a skate park, and an underground music store. Despite the furor it would cause, I'd even love to have one of my friends run a tattoo and piercing parlor from there.

To help increase awareness about our ministry and what we do, I've been working on a compilation CD that will include bands like the Misfits, a legendary punk-rock group. Traditional sermons and services are simply not reaching my generation. There are few if any national hosts of religious television in their twenties. The old boys don't want to let them in, but the old boys don't speak a language that kids will ever hear. These musicians do. So strange as it may seem, they're filling the void coming from the pulpit with music and lyrics that speak to a younger, more extreme audience.

In that same vein, we continue to hold concerts featuring Christian as well as non-Christian bands. At one such performance, a father who had brought his two kids rebuked me for playing a non-Christian CD containing bad language during the intermission.

"You need to take this music off," he demanded. "There's cussing and profanity, and I'm offended. I've got kids in there."

"We're not here to entertain Christians," I finally told him after pulling off the CD and apologizing. "We're here to reach out to people, meet them wherever they're at, and show them who Jesus is. Unlike many churches, we hope to give them grace instead of judgment."

By the end of our conversation, I think he saw where I was coming from. Others, however, have been harder to convince.

These days, recordings routinely fall victim to Christian censors. All too often, Christian artists get condemned for content deemed inappropriate or for a perceived lack of Christian lyrics. Then their material is simply banned.

In the spring of 2000, I got invited to address the Gospel Music Association's annual convention, where at least a thousand Christian music labels and store owners had come together. Though I felt nervous, I didn't hold back.

"You have to stop banning these CDs," I told them. "You will carry a thousand books that contradict each other, but you won't carry a Christian album because it says the word 'suck.' You blank out covers like the one on the newest release by P.O.D. [the strongest, most relevant Christian band I know, who are on MTV and who are preaching the gospel in some of the country's darkest spots] just because it looks like a Salvador Dali painting. Why aren't we supporting these people who are going into territories we've never been and reaching people who have never been reached before? Kids are dying and going to hell every day, and a lot of these bands are the only Jesus they will ever see.

"You still want to know why you're not reaching today's youth?" I concluded. "My generation is trying to minister in its own way, and you're not letting us."

In the midst of an ecclesiastic vacuum for young people, God has given me a voice and is putting my life back together. I'm even starting to see the restoration in my life reflected in my parents' as well.

My dad is restoring ministers at his home. Through his new ministry, Morningside, any burned-out minister can stay there free of charge to relax and recharge. Dad is also building a retreat center for inner-city youth so they have a place to stay while getting their lives back together. Dad even has a vision that may land him back on television, for despite being beaten down, he remains a natural-born leader and one of the hardest working men I've ever seen in my life. He remains my hero.

Mom has already returned to the screen—the big one this time—with her documentary *The Eyes of Tammy Faye,* which has been acclaimed by everybody from the Sundance Film Festival to New York's audiences and critics. Now an ordained minister who preaches God's love and acceptance, she goes where no other evangelist can—straight to Hollywood and prime time, on TV series like *Roseanne* and the *Drew Carey Show.* She retains the wild, fun, crazy streak that makes her so unique and revels in being a wife to Roe, a mother to my sister and me, and a grandmother to my nephews, James and Jonathan. She has never been afraid to be herself despite all the criticism and scorn, which has always encouraged me to be who I am, tattoos, piercings, and all. Her greatest quality remains her ability to laugh at herself and not take life too seriously. That's obviously a lesson I'm still trying to learn.

And Tammy Sue, who has long been ignored by the Christian music industry because of her name and despite her incomparable voice, is about to get a record deal. Despite all the cruelty, which caused her such tremendous financial and emotional suffering, she continues to be the most amazing mother and a treasured confidant who has helped bring me through this whole ordeal and make me the man I am today.

Yes, the Bakkers are finally being restored.

Though God restores better than any human ever could, the church needs to start helping with that process again. As Christians, we're supposed to be grace-givers. We're supposed to be restorers. So when we see pastors fall, we need to run to them and pick them up instead of further beating them down. As Galatians 6:1–3 directs, when we see hurting people, we need to love them no matter what, because we're all struggling with something.

We've got to stop giving up on people so easily and realize that, as a church, barring extreme circumstances like those in which someone is harming others, we should never kick anyone out. In short, we have to get back to the cross, back to God, who gave up His rights as a divine being to walk this earth as a man for us and who died on a cross to make us holy and blameless in His eyes.

Traditional religion has set an impossible standard for us to achieve and then bases God's love on that standard. That screws everyone up, because, inside, even the guys who are preaching it are dying of guilt and fear. Let's face it. People are not robots that can be programmed to be perfect Christians. We're all sinners. We all have shameful moments we don't want people to know about. And whether we transgress through action or thought, Jesus knows full well that none of us are perfect. Indeed, why would we need Him if we were?

Ironically, our fear of sin actually holds us hostage to it. In Romans 7:8 it says that the law only arouses your passion more. So it was with me. Only after I finally figured out that God loved me despite my drinking and that He would love me just as much whether I drank my whole life or quit the next day did I find the strength to stop. The knowledge of His acceptance is what finally allowed me to get sober. When I was secure in God's love for me, my battle with alcohol eased, and I started to lose the tendency and even the desire to sin.

I've got friends who are struggling to the death with substance-abuse problems. As with all sin, they will eventually be forced to pay the human consequences. But that doesn't affect God's grace, because Christ came to call all sinners, not just the neat, cute ones.

As a pastor, I obviously don't give people a license to sin. But I don't condemn them. I don't diminish their problems or tell people to get over them. I tell them to get through them, to realize that their problems have a purpose, and that God's love and acceptance will help bring them around. My goal is to restore those around me and help them find peace in their lives. I don't know if some of my friends will ever live up to so-called church-going standards. But they love Jesus and have a relationship with Him. And I know I'll be sitting in heaven with them just as much as with anybody else.

It's simple. Jesus loves you for who you are, not who you

can become. But we still have such a long way to go when it comes to sharing that message.

"How come you never told me about grace?" I asked Mike Wall toward the end of 1999, almost five years after starting out with him in Phoenix.

"I never knew what it was," he confessed.

Therein lies my true life's calling: To show others that Jesus really loves them no matter who they are or what they've done. I'm not saying that everything is going to be perfect, because our relationship with Jesus is not always easy. If you pray for faith, you're going to have to go through some hard times, because you're going to learn how to have faith. If you pray for patience, you can be sure that God will test you until you develop that very quality.

But I am saying that religion as it now stands is a killer. We've got to abandon the rhetoric that God's love is conditional and get back to Jesus. Reaching people with this message will take more than music, bands—no matter how hard-core—or even preaching. It takes time. The more we encourage people to have a personal relationship with Jesus and the more transparent we can become with one another about *our* failures, faults, and struggles, the stronger the church will become.

If we don't, we will continue to lose the very people we want to attract to Christ. So many people don't know the Lord—and don't want to—because they see the lack of love and the lack of forgiveness that so many churches have shown. They're driven away by the condemnation and the infighting within the church, by a religion that instead of preaching grace is known as the only army that kills its wounded.

God, however, gave me a grasp of grace. I now know that I had to go through all those trials to fulfill God's purpose for me, to bring the message of Christ's unconditional love to the saved and unsaved alike. Through the résumé of my life, which has been so painfully public—and publicly painful—I've experienced firsthand how much the church needs to change if we're to bring that message to new generations.

Sometimes God has to break your heart to open it. That's what He did with me. And with His help, I came through everything strong enough to launch a revolution. Although my Revolution may fade away, I will continue to show those who have been labeled as outcasts that Jesus loves them unconditionally, no matter what. Though people will tend to hate and fight this, struggling and squiggling all the way because they've heard the opposite message for so long, in the end that approach will win them over to Christ.

So maybe the dream that lay behind Heritage USA didn't crumble after all. Maybe it simply changed, because the dream never lay in those buildings—it lay in reaching people for Christ and showing them His love.

And that revolution will never die.

Index